# Courtney

## VOLUME TWO

# Crumrin

## The Coven of Mystics

Written & Illustrated by

—❖— TED NAIFEH —❖—

Colored by

### WARREN WUCINICH

Original Series edited by
**JAMES LUCAS JONES**

Collection edited by
**JILL BEATON**

Design by
**KEITH WOOD**

Oni Press, Inc.

*publisher,* JOE NOZEMACK

*editor in chief,* JAMES LUCAS JONES

*director of marketing,* CORY CASONI

*art director,* KEITH WOOD

*operations director,* GEORGE ROHAC

*editor,* JILL BEATON

*editor,* CHARLIE CHU

*digital prepress lead,* TROY LOOK

Originally published as issues 1-4 of the Oni Press comic series
*Courtney Crumrin and the Coven of Mystics.*

1305 SE Martin Luther King Jr. Blvd.
Suite A
Portland, OR 97214

www.onipress.com

First Edition: August 2012

ISBN 978-1-934964-80-4

1 3 5 7 9 10 8 6 4 2

Library of Congress Control Number: 2011933144

Printed in China.

*For Kelly*

'ILLSBOROUGH'S A SAFE PLACE TO RAISE YER *KIDDIES*, SO LONG AS THEY *KNOW* TO STAY OUT O' THE *WOODS*.

*NASTY* THINGS LURKIN' ABOUT.

LIKE *ME*, FER INSTANCE!

SQUEEE!

*MOST* O' THE LITTLE TYKES LEARN TO KEEP *AWAY*.

BUT YOUNG *COURTNEY CRUMRIN*, SHE'S A DIFFERENT *STORY*.

*WILLFUL* LASS.

SHE THINKS SHE'S GOT THE *BETTER* O' OL' *BUTTERWORM*.

SUPPOSE SHE'S *RIGHT*, TOO.

A GIRL WITH 'ER POWERS GOT NOTHIN' TO *FEAR* FROM AN OL' BUG-A-BOO LIKE ME.

*COURSE*, THERE'S ALWAYS A *BIGGER* BUG-A-BOO.

# Chapter One

HEAR ME, DARK AND *DREADFUL* ONES, *HORRENDOUS* CHILDREN 'NEATH *COLD STONE.*

RELEASE THY *MOST ACCURSED* SON, TO SERVE MY *NEED* AND MINE *ALONE.*

AWAKEN, FIEND FROM DEPTHS UNKNOWN, I *BID* THEE, *RISE FROM SUNLESS LANDS,*

TO RENDER *FLESH* FROM *BLOODY BONE,*

TO FEAST ON *GORE* AT *MY COMMAND.*

HEH HEH.

YEH SHOULD'VE BEEN *FASTER,* BROTHER.

》ULP《

OH BUGGER!

"MISS *CRUMRIN?*"

HMM!

WHA'!?!

I'M SORRY TO BORE YOU, MISS CRUMRIN.

BUT SURELY AMERICAN HISTORY ISN'T THAT DULL.

MUST BE THE WAY YOU TEACH IT THEN...

WHAT WAS THAT?

SORRY, STAYED UP LATE. HOMEWORK.

I SEE.

CRUMRIN

UNDER THE CIRCUMSTANCES I CAN ONLY BE SO SYMPATHETIC.

WHAT'S THIS!?!

A ZERO.

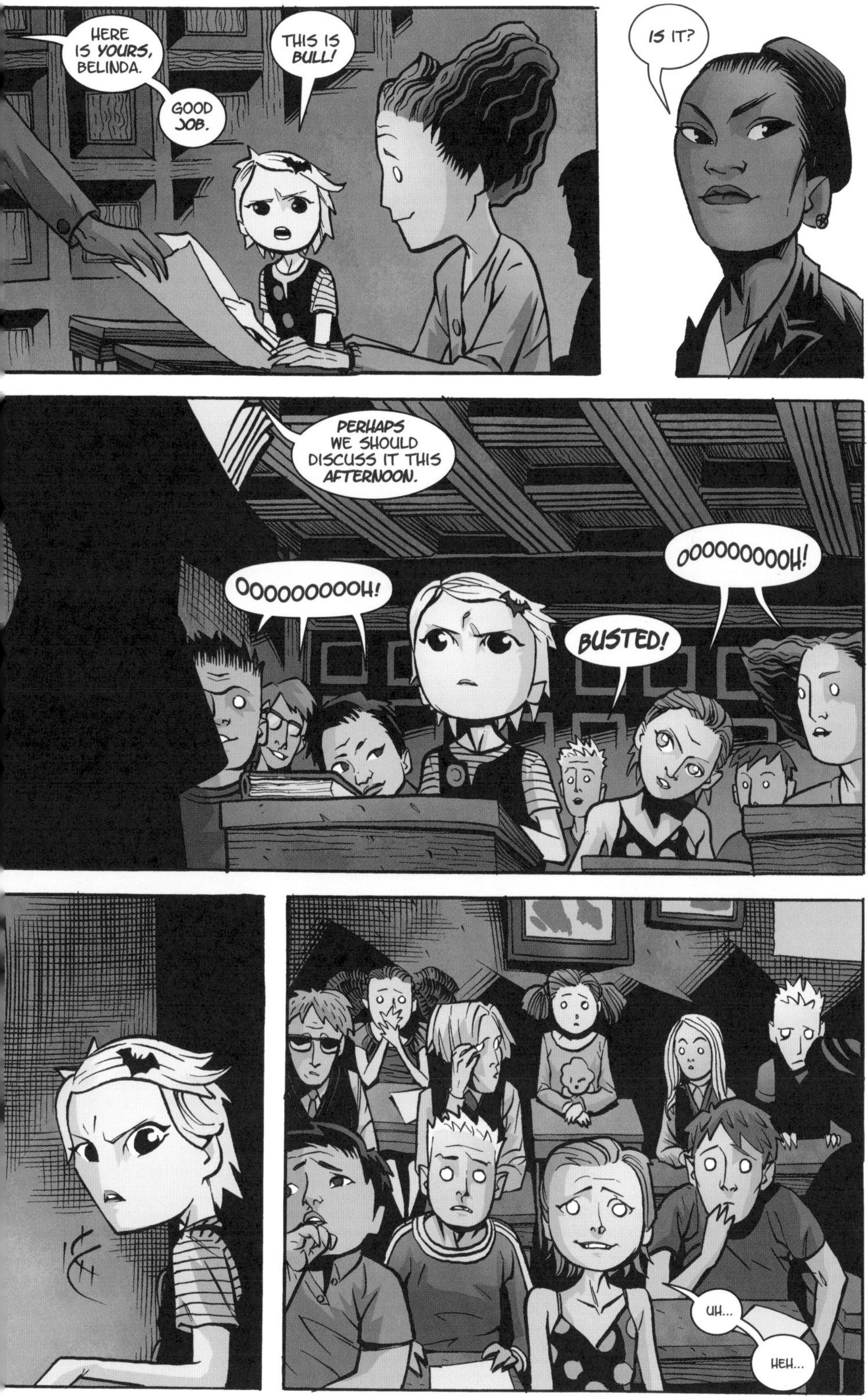
HERE IS YOURS, BELINDA.
GOOD JOB.
THIS IS BULL!
IS IT?
PERHAPS WE SHOULD DISCUSS IT THIS AFTERNOON.
OOOOOOOOOH!
BUSTED!
OOOOOOOOOH!
UH...
HEH...

IT WAS NOW TWO WEEKS INTO THE NEW SCHOOL YEAR, AND COURTNEY WAS BEGINNING TO NOTICE THAT HER NEW TEACHER, MISS CRISP, WAS A DREADFUL NUISANCE.

THERE WAS NOTHING WRONG WITH THE HOMEWORK, OF COURSE. THE COMPLEX COCKTAIL OF ENCHANTMENTS HAD REQUIRED WEEKS OF RESEARCH, BUT NOW A BEWITCHED BELINDA BLOOM HANDED IN TWO COPIES OF HOMEWORK EVERY DAY, ONE WITH COURTNEY'S NAME ON IT.

THE ENSORCELLED GIRL NEVER EVEN REALIZED SHE WAS DOING IT. AND COURTNEY WAS NOW FREE TO DEVOTE HER FULL ATTENTION TO HER GROWING OBSESSION, HER UNCLE'S LIBRARY OF WITCHCRAFT.

SHE HAD NO INTENTION OF ALLOWING THIS MEDDLESOME WOMAN TO RUIN THINGS.

I HAPPEN TO *KNOW* THAT PAPER WAS *PERFECT*.

I HAD MY *PARENTS* DOUBLE-*CHECK* IT.

EXIT

OF *COURSE* IT WAS PERFECT. BELINDA'S HOMEWORK IS *ALWAYS* EXEMPLARY.

THE *IDEA* IS FOR YOU TO DO IT *YOURSELF*, AND ACTUALLY *LEARN* SOMETHING.

*YOU* THINK *BELINDA* DID MY HOMEWORK FOR ME? SHE DOESN'T EVEN *LIKE* ME.

YOU HAVE TO HAVE *FRIENDS* TO CHEAT THAT WAY.

OR *OTHER* POWERS OF PERSUASION.

I... DON'T KNOW WHAT YOU'RE *TALKING* ABOUT.

YOU THINK I'M *BLACKMAILING—*

*COURTNEY,* I HAPPEN TO *KNOW* YOU'RE GETTING AN *EXCELLENT* EDUCATION FROM YOUR *UNCLE.*

*HOWEVER,* THERE ARE CERTAIN THINGS YOU'RE *NOT* GOING TO LEARN FROM *HIM,* AND YOU'LL *NEED* THEM TO LIVE IN THE *ORDINARY* WORLD.

DO YOU *UNDERSTAND?*

...

*YES,* MS. CRISP.

*SCREW* THE ORDINARY WORLD.

OVER THE LAST YEAR, COURTNEY CRUMRIN HAD SETTLED COMFORTABLY INTO HILLSBOROUGH. SHE FOUND THAT, GENERALLY, THE ENVIRONMENT WAS TO HER LIKING.

SHE'D MADE FEW FRIENDS AMONG THE LOCAL CHILDREN, AND THAT ALSO WAS TO HER LIKING, FOR THEY WERE NOT.

WHAT'ER YEH DOIN' IN THE *WOODS*, LASS?

ARE YEH *THAT* DAFT?

YOU TRYING TO SCARE ME, BUTTERWORM?

I EAT SPOOKS LIKE *YOU* FOR *BREAKFAST*.

THAT *SO* NOW?

WELL, *I* AIN'T ONE T' BE TELLIN' A *POWERFUL WITCH* THE LIKES O' YOU WHAT'S WHAT.

BUT THE STRANGE OLD NEIGHBORHOOD WAS AT LAST BEGINNING TO FEEL LIKE HOME.

THE FOREST STIRRED SUDDENLY, AND COURTNEY FELT AN AWFUL THRILL TICKLE HER SPINE.

SOMETHING WAS COMING.

YEH JUST KEEP ON *GOIN'* THEN, LASS.

BUT YEH *MIGHT* FIND A SPOOK THAT *STICKS* IN YER *THROAT* A BIT.

SOMETHING... UNSPEAKABLE.

WHATEVER IT WAS SOON PASSED BY, BUT COURTNEY HUDDLED IN THE UNDERGROWTH FOR AN HOUR AND SHIVERED UNCONTROLLABLY.

NOW HER ONLY THOUGHT WAS TO REACH HER UNCLE.

A RICH HELPING OF DREAD AND HORROR HAD BEEN STUFFED DOWN HER THROAT.

HER INSIDES WERE STILL WRITHING FROM THE EXPERIENCE, AND SHE BARELY NOTICED THE STRANGE MEN ON THE DOORSTEP.

EXCUSE ME, MISS.

WE'RE LOOKING FOR PROFESSOR CRUMRIN.

UNCLE A, I NEED TO *TALK* TO YOU.

COME IN, MY DEAR.

GENTLEMEN.

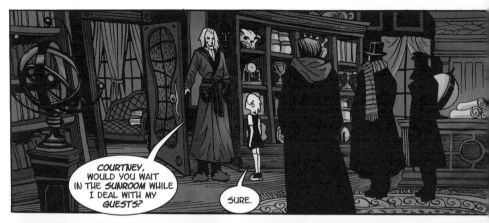

COURTNEY, WOULD YOU WAIT IN THE *SUNROOM* WHILE I DEAL WITH MY *GUESTS?*

SURE.

UNCLE ALOYSIUS RARELY HAD VISITORS, AND NEVER ENCOURAGED THEM TO LINGER.

COURTNEY KNEW THERE MUST BE OTHER WARLOCKS, BUT UP TILL NOW, SHE HADN'T MET ANY.

SHE WASN'T SURE SHE LIKED THE LOOK OF THEM.

I UNDERSTAND YOUR *RELUCTANCE,* BUT *FRANKLY,* MY DEAR FELLOW, THERE'S NO ONE ELSE WITH YOUR *EXPERTISE.*

WHAT ABOUT MADAM *HARKEN?*

SHE KNOWS AS MUCH OF THESE MATTERS AS *I.* PERHAPS MORE.

PERHAPS.

BUT THE *COMMITTEE* HAS FAR MORE CONFIDENCE IN YOU.

I'M HONORED.

EXCELLENT. SO IT'S SETTLED.

INDEED. THANK YOU FOR *THINKING* OF ME.

I HOPE YOUR *NEXT* CHOICE PROVES MORE *FRUITFUL.*

YOU DON'T SEEM TO *APPRECIATE* THE *GRAVITY* OF THIS MATTER, ALOYSIUS.

PROFESSOR, WHAT ABOUT THE *MANDRAKES?* JACK AND THE CHILDREN?

JACK MANDRAKE, THE SELF-PROCLAIMED *GREATEST* WARLOCK OF THE AGE?

SURELY HE *ISN'T* IN ANY DANGER.

HAVE YOU NOT *HEARD?*

PROFESSOR, THEY'RE DEAD.

LAST *NIGHT.*

THE CHILDREN AS WELL?

*HECTOR* HERE IS DOING HIS *BEST,* BUT HE *JUST* ISN'T EQUIPPED TO DEAL WITH... *YOU KNOW...*

*NIGHT* THINGS.

NOT LIKE *THIS* ONE.

I JUST WANTED TO *TELL* YOU THAT...

I SAW *SOMETHING*. OUT IN THE *WOODS*.

WHEN THEY'D GONE, ALOYSIUS CAME TO SPEAK WITH COURTNEY. HE LOOKED OLD AND, FOR THE FIRST TIME THAT COURTNEY NOTICED, A BIT FRAIL.

*NOW* THEN, COURTNEY, WHAT WAS THE *TROUBLE?*

SOMETHING *BAD.*

COURTNEY, I DON'T WANT YOU *GOING* INTO THE *WOODS* FOR A WHILE.

WHAT'S *OUT* THERE?

NOTHING YOU NEED TO *KNOW* ABOUT.

*BUTTERWORM!*

BUT COURTNEY CRUMRIN, AS YOU CAN WELL IMAGINE, WAS THE SORT OF PERSON THAT FELT SHE NEEDED TO KNOW EVERYTHING.

C'MON, BUTTERWORM.

DON'T *MAKE* ME GET MY DAD'S ELECTRIC CLIPPERS.

WHAT YEH WANT?

AND *KEEP* YER VOICE DOWN, GIRL, FER *GOODNESS* SAKE.

WHAT *IS* IT, BUTTERWORM? WHAT'S *OUT* THERE?

COURTNEY WISHED FOR SOME DAYS AFTERWARD SHE HADN'T ASKED. IT SEEMED THERE WERE SOME THINGS SHE DIDN'T NEED TO KNOW AFTER ALL.

THE GOBLIN SMILED ITS NASTY LITTLE SMILE.

AND THEN IT TOLD COURTNEY ABOUT THE WORST HOBGOBLIN THAT EVER WAS.

OH, 'IM? THAT'S OL' TOMMY *RAWHEAD.*

BEEN *AWHILE* SINCE HE COME OUT O' THE *MARL-PIT.*

TOMMY *RAWHEAD*?

WHO IS HE?

"WE *GOBLINS* BEEN AROUND A *LONG* TIME. SOME ARE *BAD*, LIKE *ME*. SOME ARE *WORSE*."

"OL' *TOMMY*, HE'S THE WORST OF *ALL*."

FOR HEAVEN'S *SAKE*, CHARLES. YOU'RE UPSETTING THE *CHILDREN*.

*SORRY*, DEAR.

ALRIGHT, MY LITTLE *BEASTIES*. *BEDTIME*.

"'E'S THE ONE THAT *MORTALS* ALWAYS WARNED THEIR *CHILDREN* ABOUT.

"THEY'D SAY, '*DON'T* STRAY TOO NEAR THE *MARL-PIT*, OR OL' *RAWHEAD 'N' BLOODY BONES'*LL PULL YEH *IN*.'"

CAN I SLEEP IN *YOUR* ROOM TONIGHT, DADDY?

AREN'T YOU A LITTLE OLD—?

YES!

YES, YOU *CAN*.

"BUT *THING* 'BOUT OL' *TOMMY*, *SOMETIMES* YOU DON'T *NEED* TO GO NEAR THE *MARL-PIT* TO FIND 'IM. SOMETIMES 'E *COMES OUT*."

IS THERE *REALLY* SOMEONE OUT THERE?

A *BAD* PERSON?

*WELL*, IF THERE *WAS*, THEY'D NEVER GET *IN*.

YOUR *FATHER* HAS THE HOUSE UNDER HIS *PROTECTION*.

"AN' WHEN 'E WANTS *BLOOD*, THERE'S *NOTHIN'* CAN STOP 'IM.

"NO *SPELL*, NO *CURSE*...

"NO *MAGIC*, HOWEVER *POWERFUL*, CAN *PROTECT* YEH FROM 'IM.

"AN' IF 'E *WANTS* YEH, 'E'LL 'AVE YEH. O' *THAT* YEH CAN BE *SURE*.

"'IS *ARMS* IS SO *LONG*, 'E CAN *REACH* INTO THE *FURTHEST* HIDIN' PLACES.

"'IS *FINGERS* CAN REACH UP DRAINPIPES.

"BUT THE *FUNNIEST* THING 'BOUT 'IM, EVEN *THOUGH* 'E'S A GREAT *HUGE* BUGGER..."

"'E CAN *FIT* 'ISSELF INTO THE *TEENSIEST* PLACES."

PHEW!

DANIEL!

ELLEN, STOP!

THERE'S NOTHING WE CAN DO.

"'E'S A *SLOPPY* EATER, TOMMY. *THINK* 'E LIKES 'IS MEALS T' *STRUGGLE* AND *SCREAM*."

GET YOUR *AMULET*, CHARLES.

WE'LL SEE HOW THIS BEAST LIKES THE TASTE OF THE FIRE AMULET.

AAAAAAAAHHH!!

RUN, BABY.

LET THE IMMORTAL BODIES CURSE YOU, UNCLEAN THING!

KA BOOOMMM

CURSE ME?

BUT, MY LADY, I AM ALREADY ACCURS'D ONE-HUNDRED FOLD.

"NO ONE'S EVER ESCAPED OL' RAWHEAD 'N' BLOODY BONES.

"NO ONE."

HA HA HA HA HA HA HA HA HA HA

"NOT ONCE 'E'D MADE 'IS MIND UP T' 'AVE 'EM."

COURTNEY WATCHED THE WATERY LIGHT OF MORNING SPILL INTO THE ROOM. SHE HADN'T CLOSED HER EYES ALL NIGHT.

HER BRAIN HAD NOW ACQUIRED A THICK LINTY COAT. BUT AS AWFUL AS SHE FELT...

...SHE COULD TELL THAT UNCLE ALOYSIUS FELT WORSE.

NO HOMEWORK TODAY?

THAT *WHISTLING* YOU HEAR IS THE *FALL* OF YOUR *GRADE* POINT AVERAGE.

>SNORT<

OH, YEAH. THAT WAS *ALL KINDS* O' FUNNY, WASN'T IT?

29

MS. CRISP, CAN I CHANGE SEATS?

SURE, IF ANYONE WANTS TO TRADE.

LOOK, I WASN'T FEELING TOO GOOD LAST NIGHT.

I'M NOT GOING TO GIVE YOU A ZERO THIS TIME. I IMAGINE YOU'VE BEEN WORRYING ABOUT YOUR UNCLE.

YOU'RE A WITCH, TOO, AREN'T YOU?

TAKES YOU A WHILE, BUT YOU GET THERE IN THE END.

I'M ALSO AN OLD FRIEND OF ALOYSIUS.

THEN MAYBE YOU CAN TELL ME WHAT'S GOING ON. HE SURE AS HECK HASN'T.

HMM. PERHAPS IT'S FOR THE BEST.

THAT'S **CRAP!** IF SOMETHING MIGHT **HAPPEN** TO HIM, I NEED TO **KNOW** ABOUT IT.

HE'S ALL I'VE GOT.

WHY DON'T THEY JUST LEAVE HIM **ALONE?** ISN'T HE TOO **OLD** TO BE FIGHTING **MONSTERS?**

I **THOUGHT** HE HADN'T **TOLD** YOU ANYTHING.

I'VE GOT MY **SOURCES.**

I SEE.

IT'S NOT **FAIR!**

I THOUGHT HE WAS **RETIRED** OR SOMETHING. CAN'T SOMEONE **ELSE** DEAL WITH IT?

NO ONE WANTS TO.

**ALOYSIUS** WAS **ALWAYS** THE ONE THEY ASKED TO DO THEIR **DIRTY** WORK.

HE SAYS **"YES"** BECAUSE HE **KNOWS** IT HAS TO BE DONE.

JERKS.

THAT'S THE WAY PEOPLE ARE. DO **YOU** WANT TO GO DEAL WITH IT?

THAT'S DIFFERENT.

I'M A KID.

DO YOU THINK ANY OF **THEM** FEEL MORE QUALIFIED THAN **YOU?**

THEY **DON'T.**

COURTNEY MULLED OVER MS. CRISP'S WORDS ALL THE WAY HOME. SHE TOOK THE ROAD FOR SAFETY'S SAKE, BREAKING HER LONGTIME HABIT OF CUTTING THROUGH THE FOREST.

HEY, LOOK. FRESH MEAT.

CRUMRIN.

REMEMBER?

OH. OH YEAH.

UNCLE A?

>SNFF<

COURTNEY? WHAT'S WRONG?

NOTHING.

I WAS JUST... WORRIED.

I DON'T WANT YOU TO GO OUT TONIGHT.

MY DEAR, I MUST.

WHY? IT'S NOT FAIR.

INDEED IT ISN'T.

IT'S NOT FAIR THAT THE INNOCENT SUFFER. IT'S NOT FAIR THAT CHILDREN DIE AT THE HANDS OF MONSTERS.

IT'S NOT EVEN FAIR THAT OLD MEN LIKE ME ARE FORCED OUT OF THEIR COMFORTABLE SITTING ROOMS AND INTO THE COLD NIGHT. LIFE IS OFTEN ENTIRELY UNFAIR.

BUT IT BEATS THE ALTERNATIVE.

WHAT ALTERNATIVE?

EXACTLY.

I JUST HOPE WE CAN *FIND* THE BLOODY THING BEFORE IT *HURTS* ANYONE *ELSE.*

I DON'T THINK WE HAVE TO *WORRY* ABOUT THAT, WOODRUE.

WHY NOT?

BECAUSE SOMETHING *TELLS* ME IT'S COMING *HERE.*

HMMM...

I'LL BE BACK *SOON.*

HAVE A GOOD TIME.

COURTNEY DIDN'T REALLY KNOW WHAT SHE INTENDED TO DO.

SHE HAD NO PLAN, AND COULD THINK OF NO SPELLS THAT WOULD BE OF ANY USE.

BUT SHE COULDN'T SIT IN HER BED ANOTHER NIGHT KNOWING THAT HER UNCLE WAS OUT ALONE, FACING AN UNSTOPPABLE MONSTER.

PARDON, MISS.

OF COURSE, SHE HADN'T THOUGHT SHE'D BE FACING IT ALONE HERSELF.

DO YOU LIVE IN THAT HOUSE?

ME? UH...

NO. I LIVE, UH, DOWN THE STREET.

I DIDN'T JUST SEE YOU COMING OUT THE BACK DOOR OF THAT HOUSE?

THAT ONE BEHIND YOU?

OH, YEAH, THAT HOUSE. I WAS, UH, JUST VISITING.

I SEE.

YOU WOULDN'T BE LYING TO OLD TOMMY, NOW WOULD YOU?

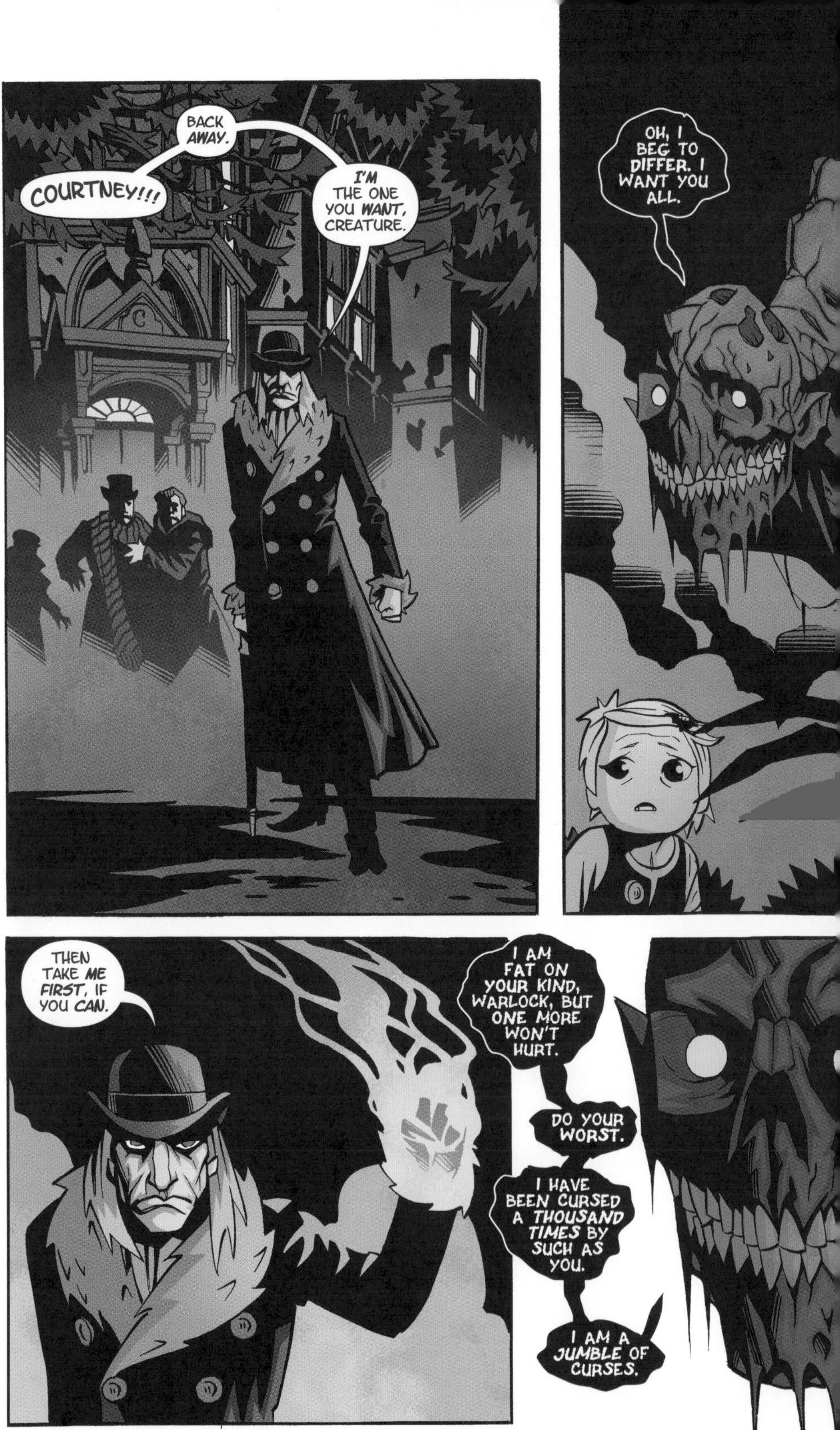
COURTNEY!!!
BACK AWAY.
I'M THE ONE YOU WANT, CREATURE.
OH, I BEG TO DIFFER. I WANT YOU ALL.
THEN TAKE ME FIRST, IF YOU CAN.
I AM FAT ON YOUR KIND, WARLOCK, BUT ONE MORE WON'T HURT.
DO YOUR WORST.
I HAVE BEEN CURSED A THOUSAND TIMES BY SUCH AS YOU.
I AM A JUMBLE OF CURSES.

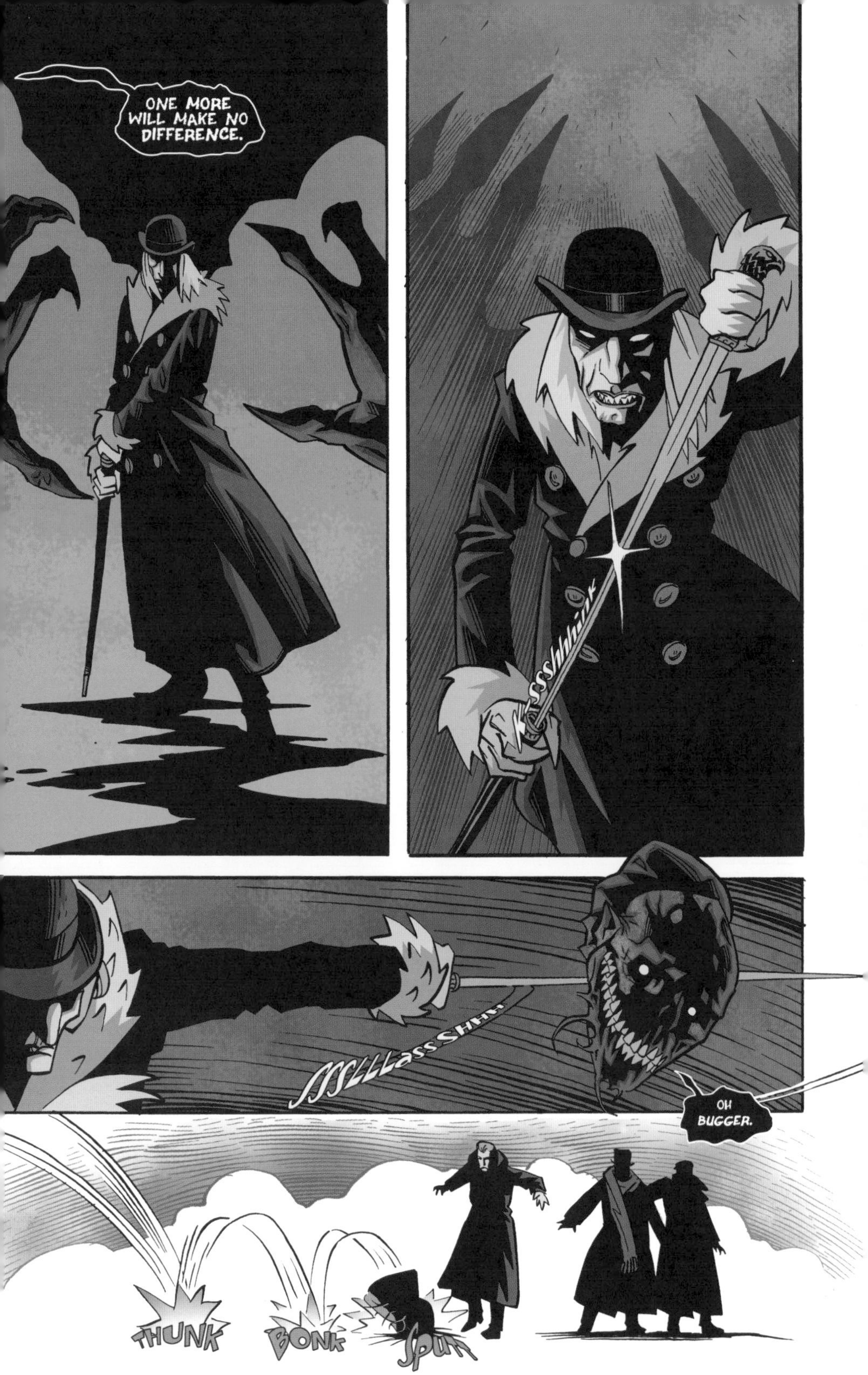
ONE MORE WILL MAKE NO DIFFERENCE.
SSSHHHIIINK
SSSLLLASSSHHH
OH BUGGER.
THUNK
BONK
SPUTT

HECTOR.

CREATURES LIKE *THIS* DON'T SIMPLY *APPEAR* AFTER A HUNDRED YEARS OF *BANISHMENT.*

SOMEONE *SUMMONED* THIS ONE, UNDOUBTEDLY FOR A *SPECIFIC PURPOSE.*

YOU *MIGHT* WANT TO LOOK INTO IT.

COURTNEY. IT'S A BIT *CHILLY* OUT.

LET'S GET INDOORS.

GENTLEMEN.

AND COURTNEY NEVER FEARED FOR UNCLE ALOYSIUS AGAIN.

# Chapter Two

HOW'S MY NIECE DOING IN SCHOOL?

GLAD TO HEAR IT.

STILL HATES ME.

IF SHE DIDN'T, YOU WOULDN'T BE DOING YOUR JOB.

THIS ISN'T A JOB, ALOYSIUS.

THIS IS A FAVOR.

OF COURSE. FORGIVE ME, MY DEAR.

GOODNESS KNOWS SHE NEEDS ALL THE HELP SHE CAN GET.

I DARESAY IF I DIDN'T STEP IN, SHE'D END UP SKULKING AROUND THAT OLD HOUSE READING MOLDY BOOKS AND FRIGHTENING THE LOCAL CHILDREN,

TOTALLY USELESS WHEN IT COMES TO ANYTHING PRACTICAL.

RATHER LIKE YOU, REALLY.

YOU FLATTER ME, CALPURNIA.

NOT AT ALL.

IT'S GETTING CHILLY.

SHALL WE GRAB A CAPPUCCINO BEFORE CALLING IT A NIGHT?

MS. CRISP WAS NOT EXAGGERATING ABOUT COURTNEY'S FEELINGS TOWARD HER. IF ANYTHING, SHE UNDERSTATED THE MATTER.

WHEN SHE REALIZED JUST HOW FAR COURTNEY HAD FALLEN BEHIND IN HER STUDIES OVER THE LAST SEVERAL MONTHS, SHE BEGAN A STRICT REGIMEN TO CATCH HER STUDENT UP.

...GRUMBLE...

COURTNEY WAS BEGINNING TO LOATHE HER.

THIS ESSAY WAS *MUCH* BETTER.

I *SUSPECTED* THERE WAS AN INTELLIGENT GIRL *SOMEWHERE* UNDERNEATH THAT SCOWL.

GEE, *THANKS.*

CAN I GO YET?

AS *SOON* AS YOU FINISH READING THAT *CHAPTER.*

I'VE GOT TO RUN SOME ERRANDS. WOULD YOU *MIND* LOCKING UP *AFTER* YOURSELF?

LEAVE THE BACK DOOR **OPEN** SO QUICK CAN GET IN AND **OUT.**

IN SOME WAYS, SCHOOLWORK WASN'T MUCH DIFFERENT THAN THE STUDY OF WITCHCRAFT. HOWEVER, WITCHCRAFT, IN COURTNEY'S OPINION, HAD FAR SUPERIOR PRACTICAL VALUE, ESPECIALLY WHEN APPLIED TO HER CLASSMATES.

NOT THAT SHE MADE A HABIT OF IT, BUT HILLSBOROUGH COULD BE QUITE DULL ON A SUNDAY AFTERNOON, AND COURTNEY HAD TO GET HER ENTERTAINMENT SOMEWHERE.

WITHER.

HMMM...

DON'T EVEN **THINK** ABOUT IT, YOUNGSTER.

QUICK WASN'T THE FIRST TALKING CAT THAT COURTNEY HAD COME ACROSS. SHE WAS BEGINNING TO SUSPECT THAT THE NEIGHBORHOOD WAS FULL OF THEM. SHE WASN'T EXACTLY AN ANIMAL PERSON, AND REGARDED CATS AS TCHOTCHKES THAT WALKED ABOUT.

BUT SHE WAS AN INQUISITIVE GIRL, AS I'VE MENTIONED BEFORE, AND HER CURIOSITY WAS PIQUED.

WHETHER A CAT CAN TALK OR NOT IS THE CAT'S BUSINESS.

IT'S NOT FOR ME TO TELL, UNLESS THE CAT IS MYSELF.

WHAT'S THE DEAL ANYWAY?

CAN ALL CATS TALK, OR WAS THERE SOME RADIATION LEAKAGE AROUND HERE OR SOMETHING?

UH-HUH. WHAT I GET FOR ASKING A CAT.

YOU CATCH ON FAST.

QUICK!

THERE YOU ARE.

WHAT'S THE HOLD-UP, GIRL? WE HAVE BUSINESS.

AH.

HELLO, MISS CRUMRIN.

HEY, BOO. WHERE ARE YOU GUYS OFF TO?

NONE OF YOUR BUSINESS.

ACTUALLY, YOU MIGHT FIND THIS INTERESTING. COME WITH US.

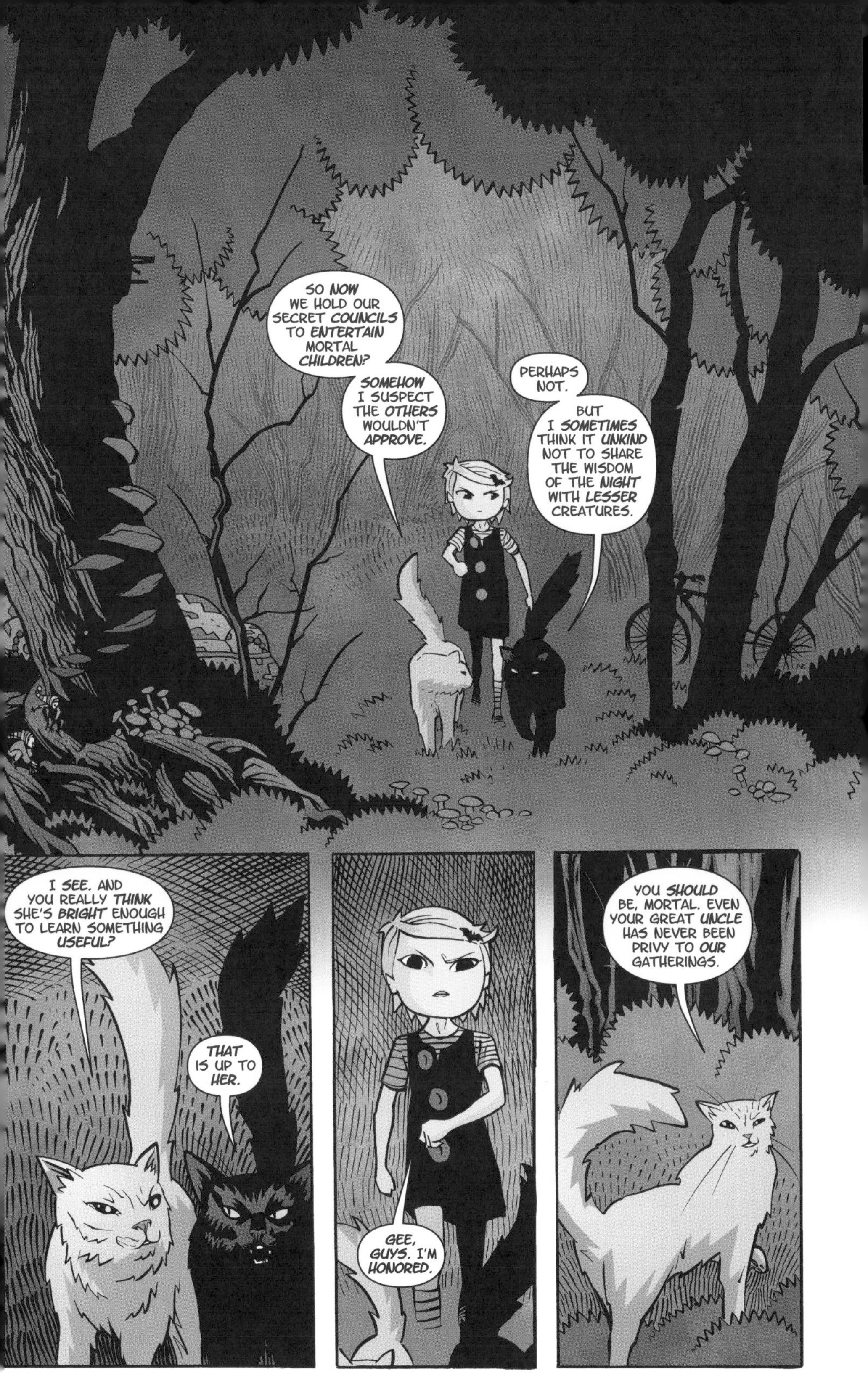
SO NOW WE HOLD OUR SECRET COUNCILS TO ENTERTAIN MORTAL CHILDREN?
SOMEHOW I SUSPECT THE OTHERS WOULDN'T APPROVE.
PERHAPS NOT.
BUT I SOMETIMES THINK IT UNKIND NOT TO SHARE THE WISDOM OF THE NIGHT WITH LESSER CREATURES.
I SEE. AND YOU REALLY THINK SHE'S BRIGHT ENOUGH TO LEARN SOMETHING USEFUL?
THAT IS UP TO HER.
GEE, GUYS. I'M HONORED.
YOU SHOULD BE, MORTAL. EVEN YOUR GREAT UNCLE HAS NEVER BEEN PRIVY TO OUR GATHERINGS.

YOU MUST EAT OF THE *PLANT* THAT GROWS IN THE SHADOW OF THIS TREE.

BUT *BEFORE* WE COME TO THE *GATHERING,* THERE'S SOMETHING YOU MUST DO, MISS CRUMRIN.

IS THERE?

HMPH. *JUST THAT? WHY?*

I DO *NOT ASK* LIGHTLY.

I CERTAINLY HAVE NO *LIKING* FOR *BRIAR* AND *BRACKEN,* THE FOOD OF MY PREY.

BUT *THIS* YOU MUST DO, OR GO *HOME.*

IT WAS AN ODD REQUEST, BUT COURTNEY WAS BY NOW FILLED WITH CURIOSITY FOR WHAT LAY AHEAD.

*MISS CRUMRIN, IS THAT* A PLANT?

HUH?

THAT'S A *FUNGUS.* IT'S QUITE POTENT, BUT I DON'T THINK YOU'D *BENEFIT* FROM ITS PROPERTIES.

I *THINK* I'LL ASK MS. CALPURNIA TO ADD *BOTANY* TO YOUR CURRICULUM.

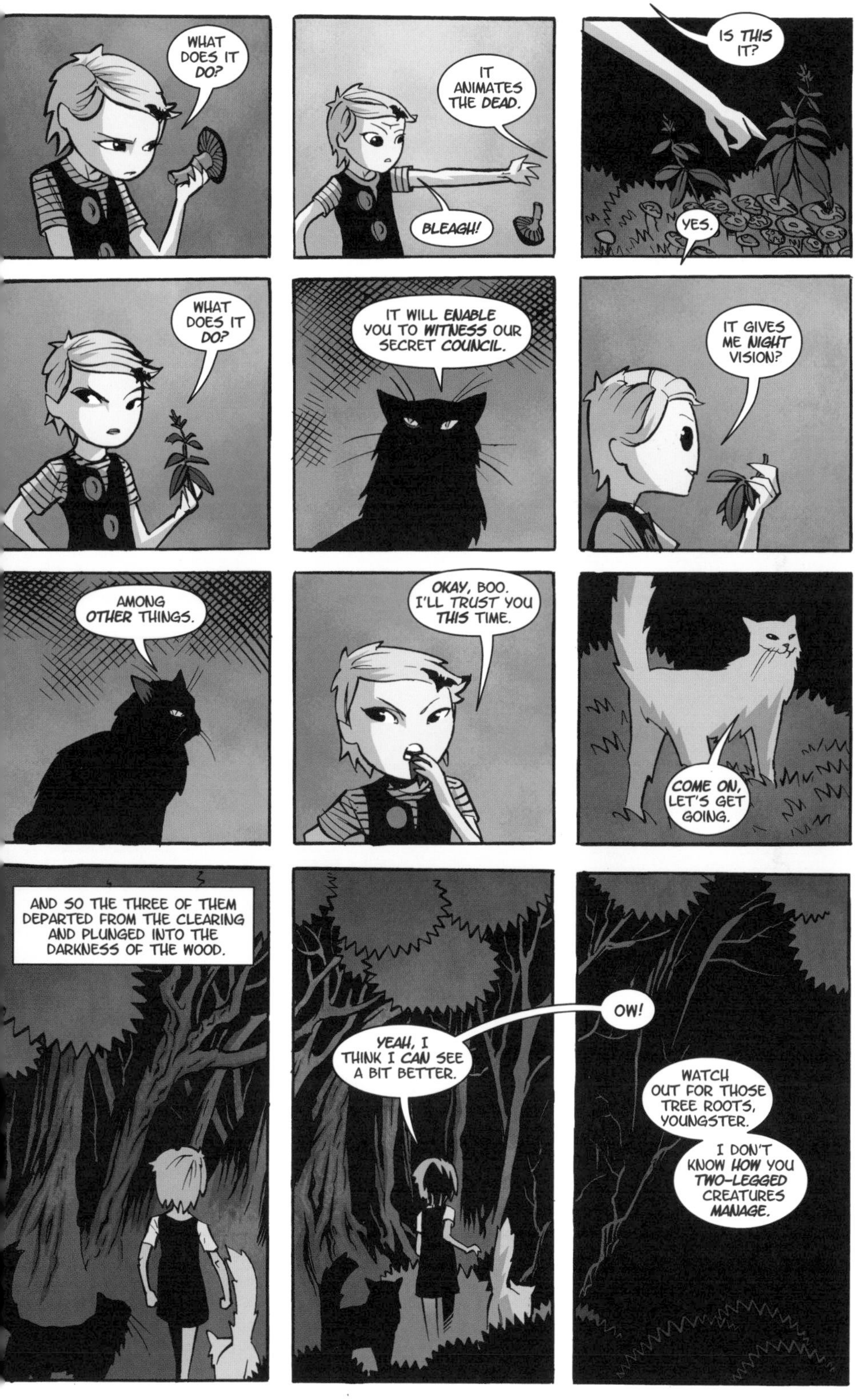

WHAT DOES IT DO?
IT ANIMATES THE DEAD.
BLEAGH!
IS THIS IT?
YES.
WHAT DOES IT DO?
IT WILL ENABLE YOU TO WITNESS OUR SECRET COUNCIL.
IT GIVES ME NIGHT VISION?
AMONG OTHER THINGS.
OKAY, BOO. I'LL TRUST YOU THIS TIME.
COME ON, LET'S GET GOING.
AND SO THE THREE OF THEM DEPARTED FROM THE CLEARING AND PLUNGED INTO THE DARKNESS OF THE WOOD.
YEAH, I THINK I CAN SEE A BIT BETTER.
OW!
WATCH OUT FOR THOSE TREE ROOTS, YOUNGSTER.
I DON'T KNOW HOW YOU TWO-LEGGED CREATURES MANAGE.

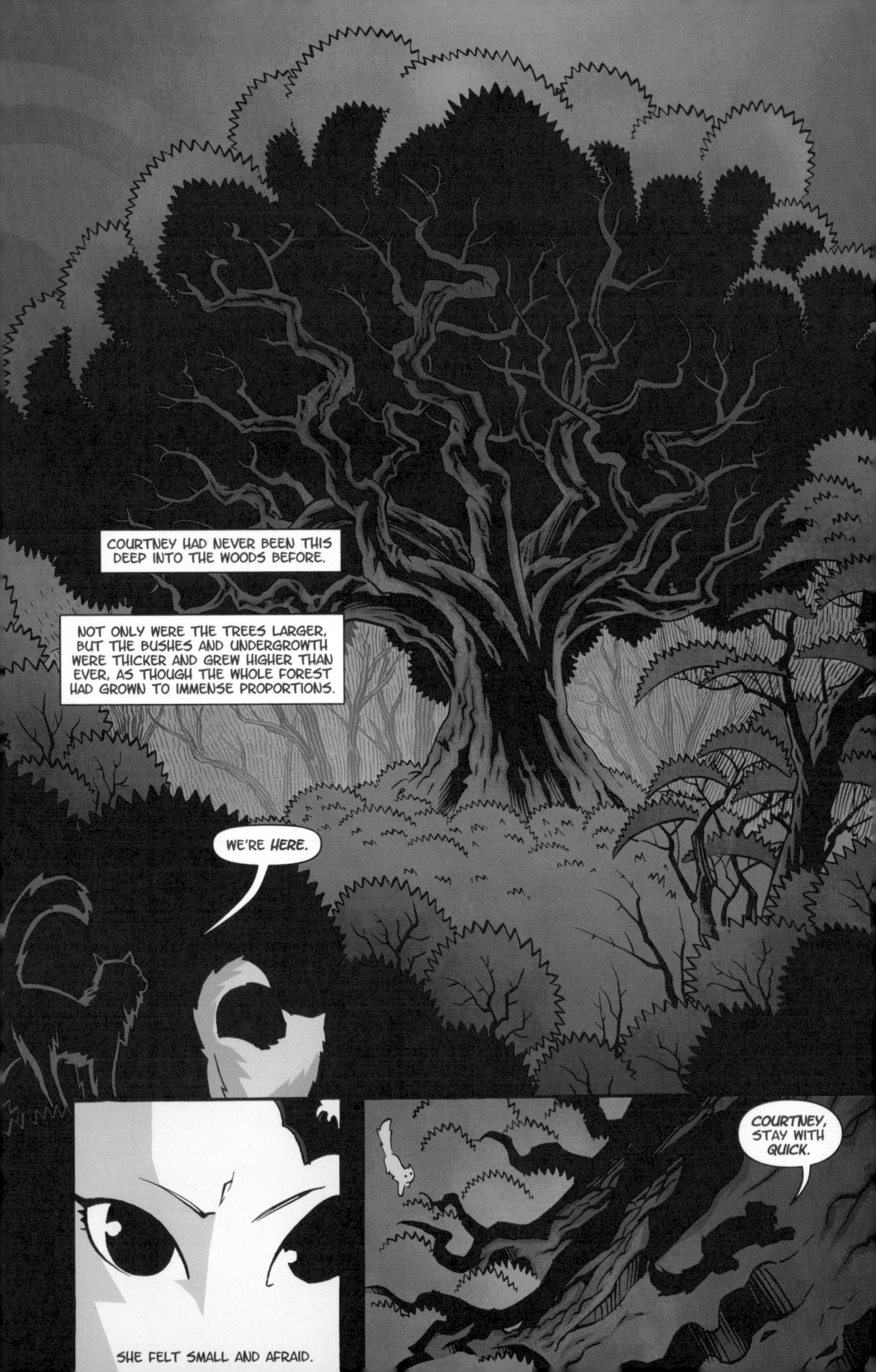
COURTNEY HAD NEVER BEEN THIS DEEP INTO THE WOODS BEFORE.
NOT ONLY WERE THE TREES LARGER, BUT THE BUSHES AND UNDERGROWTH WERE THICKER AND GREW HIGHER THAN EVER, AS THOUGH THE WHOLE FOREST HAD GROWN TO IMMENSE PROPORTIONS.
WE'RE HERE.
SHE FELT SMALL AND AFRAID.
COURTNEY, STAY WITH QUICK.

WHERE ARE THE *OTHER* CATS?

I THOUGHT YOU SAID IT WAS A *MEETING* OR A *COUNCIL* OR SOMETHING.

USE YOUR EYES.

THEY'RE ALL *AROUND* YOU.

COURTNEY FELT THE HACKLES ON THE BACK OF HER NECK RISE. THE NIGHT WAS ALIVE WITH THE FIERCE GAZE OF HUNTERS.

THEY'RE *HUGE.*

NO, CHILD. YOU'VE *SHED* A BIT OF UNNECESSARY *WEIGHT.*

*WHAT!!!* OH, YOU GOTTA BE KIDDING...

QUIET, GIRL.

DON'T *WORRY.* YOUR LARGE, LUMBERING FORM WILL *RETURN* IN THE *MORNING.*

FOR *NOW,* KEEP *SILENT.* MORTALS ARE *FORBIDDEN* HERE.

YOU'RE RISKING *MUCH* FOR YOUR ENLIGHTENMENT.

*GREAT.* THANKS FOR THE *WARNING.*

"THE BEST VIEW CAN ONLY BE HAD FROM THE MOST PRECARIOUS BOUGH."

*OLD CAT* SAYING.

*MY KINDRED.*

AT THE *BIRTH* OF *NIGHT,* I *GREET* YOU.

WHO'S *THAT?*

*TOBERMORY,* THE LEADER OF THE *PRIDES.*

IN AS MUCH AS WE HAVE LEADERS.

COURTNEY HAD NEVER SEEN SUCH A CAT. HE WAS HUGE AND SCARRED AS THOUGH FROM A THOUSAND BATTLES.

HE LOOKED AS IF HE COULD GIVE A FAIR FIGHT TO A TIMBERWOLF.

*MIDNIGHT'S CHILDREN* DO NOT GLADLY GATHER IN THIS FASHION, UNLESS SOMETHING OF GREAT *CONSEQUENCE* DRAWS THEM.

IT *HAS.*

SOME OF HIS SCARS, COURTNEY SAW, WERE FRESH, MOST NOTABLY THE ONE ACROSS HIS LEFT EYE. THE REMAINING EYE WAS STILL BRIGHT AND KEEN, AND GAZED PIERCINGLY AT THE ASSEMBLY.

I HAVE FULFILLED THE DUTIES AND REAPED THE PROFITS OF LEADERSHIP FOR TWENTY WINTERS.

LAST NIGHT, AS WAS MY DUTY, I FACED DOWN AND SLEW THE HOUND OF RADLEY HALL.

IT WAS A COSTLY VICTORY.

AS ONE, THE GATHERED ANIMALS LOWERED THEIR HEADS IN RESPECTFUL SADNESS.

EXCEPT ONE.

A LEADER MUST LEAD BY EXAMPLE.

HE MUST BE THE GREATEST HUNTER AMONG US.

UNTIL YESTERDAY, I HELD THAT DISTINCTION.

BUT A HUNTER NEEDS TWO GOOD EYES, AND I SHALL ONLY EVER SEE AGAIN OUT OF ONE.

TONIGHT, YOU MUST SELECT A NEW LEADER.

SUDDENLY THE LABYRINTHINE BRANCHES WERE ALIVE WITH THE WHISPERINGS OF CATS. THE SOUND CHILLED COURTNEY TO THE BONES. ONE WORD SEEMED TO ECHO THROUGH THE ASSEMBLY.

MITTENS.

MITTENS, GRAY AS MOONLIGHT, WHICH SEEMED TO PASS THROUGH HIM, LEAVING HIM ALMOST INVISIBLE, BUT FOR HIS WHITE PAWS.

IT'S GOING TO BE A *CLOSE THING.* BOO IS WELL REGARDED, BUT *MITTENS* IS DEADLY.

DEADLIER THAN I, THOUGH I'M FAST AS MY NAME.

PERHAPS DEADLIER THAN BOO.

COURTNEY TRIED AGAIN TO PICK HIM OUT OF THE DARKNESS.

PERHAPS.

CERTAINLY QUIETER.

WE SHALL SEE.

INDEED.

A MEMBER OF *YOUR* PRIDE, QUICK?

YES. *COURTNEY* IS HER NAME.

A *STRANGE* ODOR.

*NOT* UNPLEASANT. BUT *UNUSUAL* TO BE *SURE.* ALMOST...

*SILENCE.*

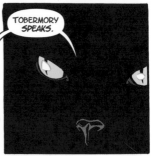

TOBERMORY *SPEAKS.*

THE HUNT BEGINS *TONIGHT.* YOU, WHO WOULD BE LEADER, MUST *KNOW* THAT TO RULE A *SINGLE CAT,* MUCH LESS ALL CATS, IS AN IMPOSSIBLE TASK.

THEREFORE, YOU MUST *SHOW* US THAT YOU ARE *EQUAL* TO IT BY HUNTING THE *UNCATCHABLE PREY.*

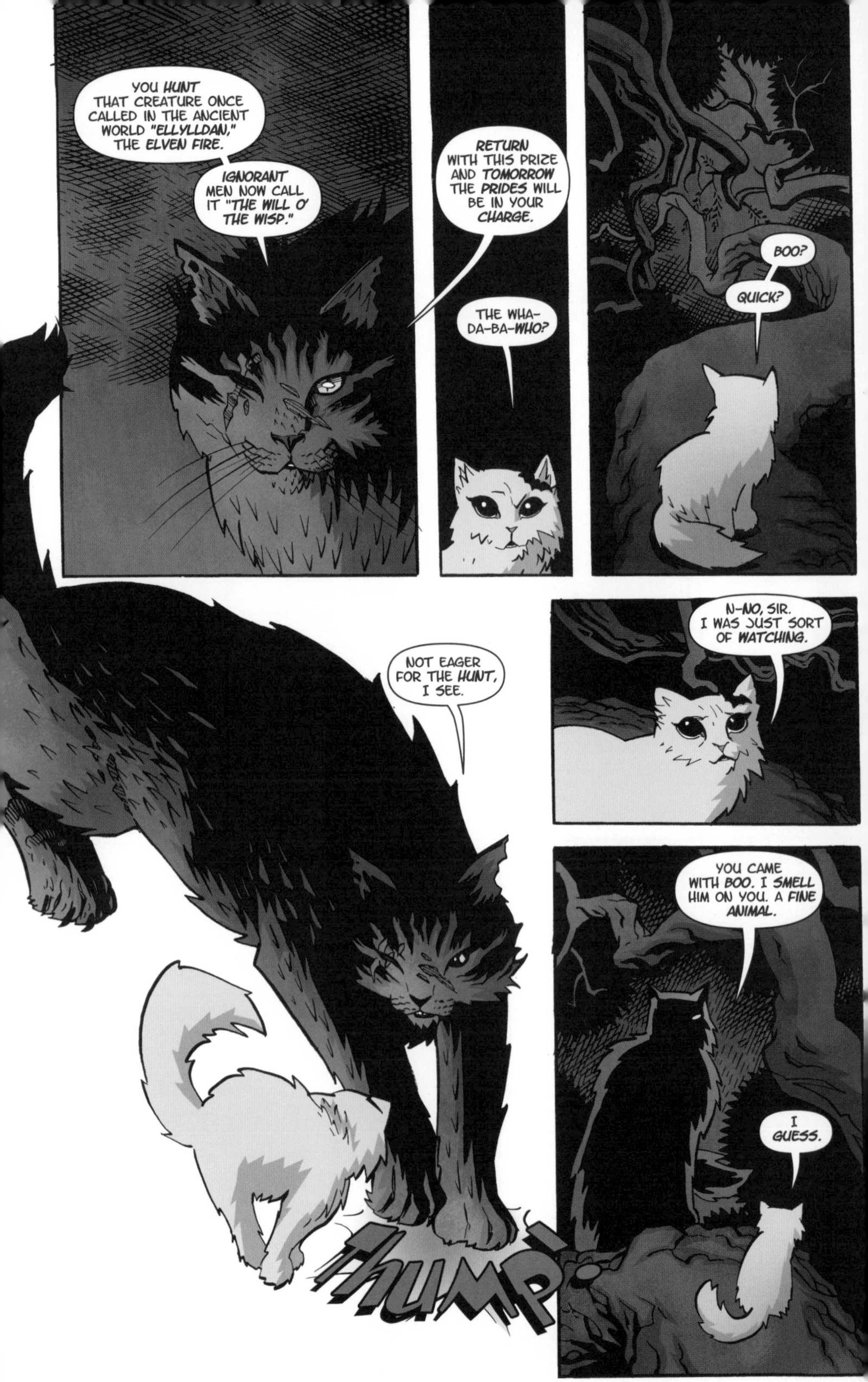
YOU HUNT THAT CREATURE ONCE CALLED IN THE ANCIENT WORLD "ELLYLLDAN," THE ELVEN FIRE.
IGNORANT MEN NOW CALL IT "THE WILL O' THE WISP."
RETURN WITH THIS PRIZE AND TOMORROW THE PRIDES WILL BE IN YOUR CHARGE.
THE WHA-DA-BA-WHO?
BOO?
QUICK?
NOT EAGER FOR THE HUNT, I SEE.
THUMP!
N-NO, SIR. I WAS JUST SORT OF WATCHING.
YOU CAME WITH BOO. I SMELL HIM ON YOU. A FINE ANIMAL.
I GUESS.

WERE IT UP TO *ME*, I'D *NAME* HIM AS MY *SUCCESSOR.*

BUT *LEADERSHIP* MUST BE *EARNED.* IT'S THE *ONLY* WAY TO PRESERVE THE *RESPECT* OF OUR KIND.

DO YOU THINK HE'LL *WIN?*

I'VE SEEN *MANY* SKILLED HUNTERS IN MY NIGHTS UPON THIS EARTH. BOO IS ONE OF THE *BEST.*

HE WOULD MAKE A *GREAT* LEADER.

BUT *HE* WILL NOT WIN.

YOU THINK *MITTENS'LL* BEAT HIM?

MITTENS IS DEADLY.

I'M *SADDENED*, FOR *ALL* WILL *SUFFER* UNDER HIS RULE.

HE IS COLD AND *CRUEL,* MORE SO THAN IS GOOD *EVEN* FOR A *CAT.*

THAT *SUCKS.*

INDEED.

BUT YOU CAME HERE TO *WATCH,* YOU SAID.

YOU'D *BETTER* MOVE *FAST,* OR YOU'LL SEE *NOTHING,* AND YOUR JOURNEY WILL BE IN *VAIN.*

SUDDENLY COURTNEY FOUND HERSELF PLUMMETING TO THE EARTH. IN A PANIC SHE TWISTED ROUND TO SEE THE GROUND COMING UP TOWARD HER.

HUH.

COOL.

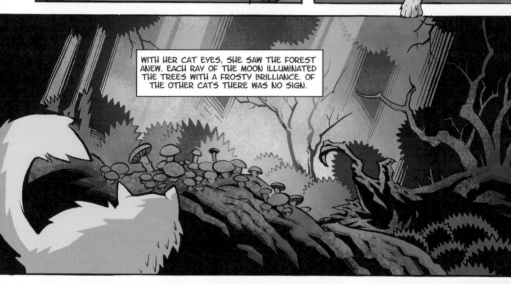

WITH HER CAT EYES, SHE SAW THE FOREST ANEW. EACH RAY OF THE MOON ILLUMINATED THE TREES WITH A FROSTY BRILLIANCE. OF THE OTHER CATS THERE WAS NO SIGN.

YET SOMETHING PROPELLED HER FORWARD; A COMPELLING SENSE WHICH LED TO BOO.

WHEN SHE FOUND HIM, HER NEWLY ACQUIRED INSTINCTS HELD HER SILENT. HE WAS PREPARING TO SPRING.

HIS PREY MUST HAVE BEEN CLOSE, BUT SHE COULDN'T AS YET SEE IT.

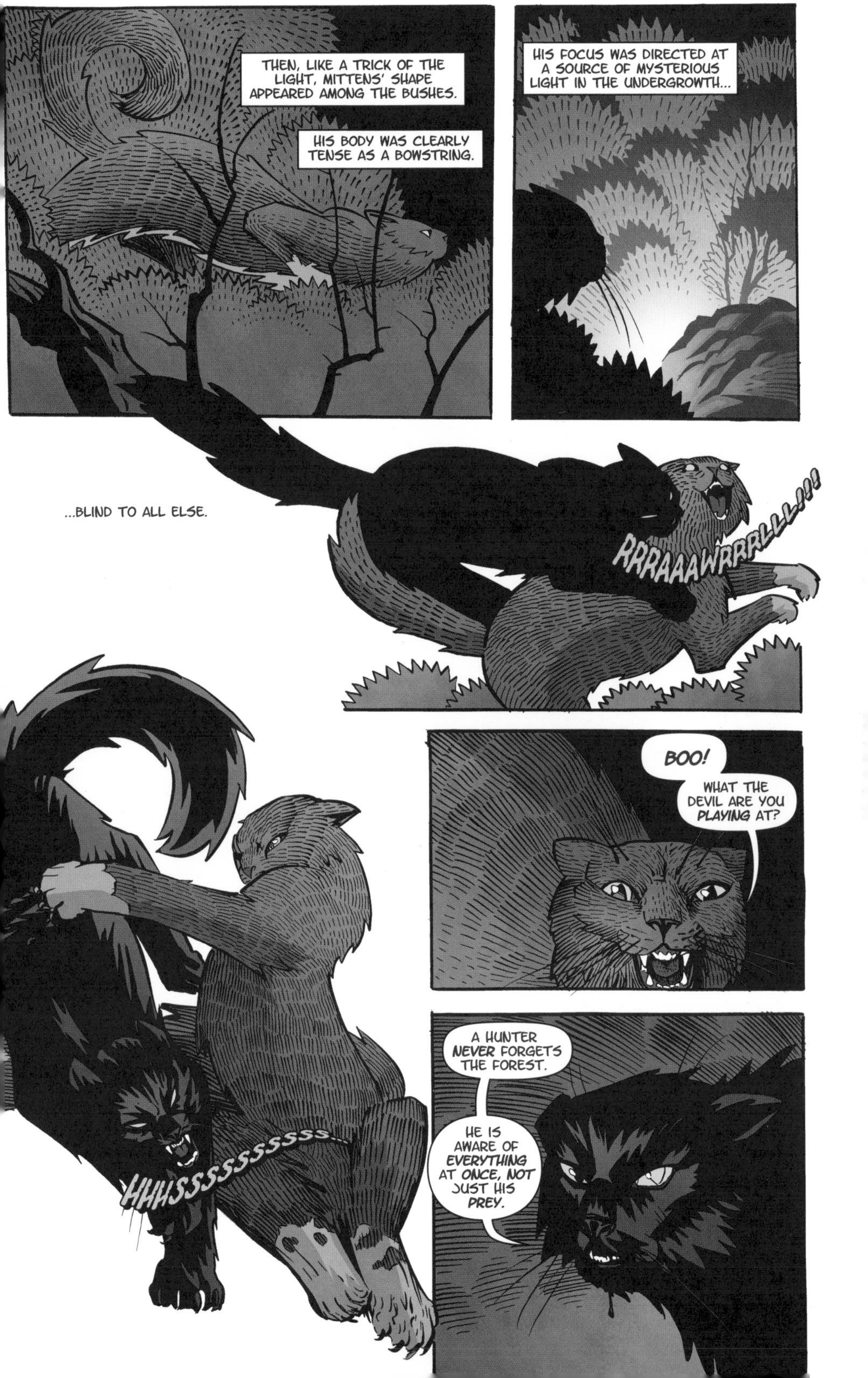
THEN, LIKE A TRICK OF THE LIGHT, MITTENS' SHAPE APPEARED AMONG THE BUSHES.
HIS BODY WAS CLEARLY TENSE AS A BOWSTRING.
HIS FOCUS WAS DIRECTED AT A SOURCE OF MYSTERIOUS LIGHT IN THE UNDERGROWTH...
...BLIND TO ALL ELSE.
RRRAAAWRRRLLLL!!!
HHHSSSSSSSSSSSSSS...
BOO!
WHAT THE DEVIL ARE YOU PLAYING AT?
A HUNTER NEVER FORGETS THE FOREST.
HE IS AWARE OF EVERYTHING AT ONCE, NOT JUST HIS PREY.

TRUE. I SHALL NOT FORGET AGAIN.

THEN HE MELTED INTO THE NIGHT.

YOU OKAY?

YES, BUT NOW HE'LL MORE EASILY SMELL MY COMING.

SHOULDN'T YOU BE TRYING TO CATCH THE THING YOURSELF?

PERHAPS. I CERTAINLY SHOULDN'T BE SITTING HERE LICKING MY WOUNDS.

FAREWELL.

BOO SLIPPED LIKE A SHADOW INTO THE DARKNESS, LEAVING COURTNEY ALONE ONCE AGAIN.

JUST AS SHE RESOLVED TO FOLLOW, SHE HEARD STRANGE NOISES.

THE FOREST, THOUGH ALIVE WITH CATS DASHING BACK AND FORTH, NEVER VISIBLE FOR MORE THAN A SECOND, HAD BEEN SILENT UP TILL NOW.

SUCH A TERRIFIC CLAMOR SHATTERED THE SILENCE THAT SHE WAS CONVINCED A BULLDOZER WAS MOVING THROUGH THE TREES.

THEN SHE HEARD VOICES.

HUMAN VOICES.

THERE. DO YOU SEE THE TRACK?

THE BEAST CAN'T BE FAR. THE UNDERBRUSH IS STILL MOVING.

COURTNEY TRIED TO SUPPRESS HERSELF, BUT BY THEN HER NERVES WERE ON EDGE.

RAERRRR!

WAS THAT IT?

NO, BUT I'LL WAGER IT'S NEAR.

THERE.

THE FOREST IS FULL OF CATS TONIGHT, BUT THAT'S THE FIRST ONE I'VE HEARD.

SOMETHING STARTLED IT.

THE HUGE MEN CRASH OFF THROUGH THE BUSHES LIKE ELEPHANTS. COURTNEY KNEW THAT SHE'D LEAD THEM RIGHT TO THEIR QUARRY, AND DIDN'T FEEL GOOD ABOUT IT. HER INQUISITIVENESS UNQUENCHED, SHE RESOLVED TO FOLLOW.

,Snap?

WHAT WAS THAT!?!

IT'S THAT KITTEN AGAIN.

GONE. BLAST IT.

THEY CRASHED AWAY AGAIN.

>SCRITCHK
>SCRITCHK

COURTNEY WENT RIGID AS SHE TURNED TO MEET THE GAZE OF THE CREATURE. WHAT SHE SAW IN ITS EYES GAVE HER PAUSE.

THEN IT DEFTLY PLUNGED BACK INTO THE FOREST.

COURTNEY WAS QUITE ASTOUNDED. SHE'D MET MANY CREATURES OF THE NIGHT, BEFRIENDED A FEW, BEEN CHARMED BY SOME, REPELLED BY OTHERS. SHE'D NEVER REALLY CONSIDERED BEFORE WHETHER ANY OF THEM HAD A SOUL.

LOOKING INTO THIS ONE'S EYES, SHE HAD NO DOUBT.

FILLED WITH WONDER, SHE DETERMINED TO MEET IT AGAIN.

ITS SCENT WAS SWEET AND MUSKY IN HER NOSTRILS, AND BEFORE LONG SHE FOUND IT...

...CROUCHING BY A CLEAR STREAM TO QUENCH ITS THIRST.

THEN SHE HEARD THE DREADFUL SOUND OF A HUMAN VOICE.

GOT YOU NOW, YOU FOUL THING.

COURTNEY KNEW SHE HAD LESS THAN A SECOND TO ACT. SHE TURNED AND DASHED AT THE HUNTER, LEAPING TO THE ATTACK.

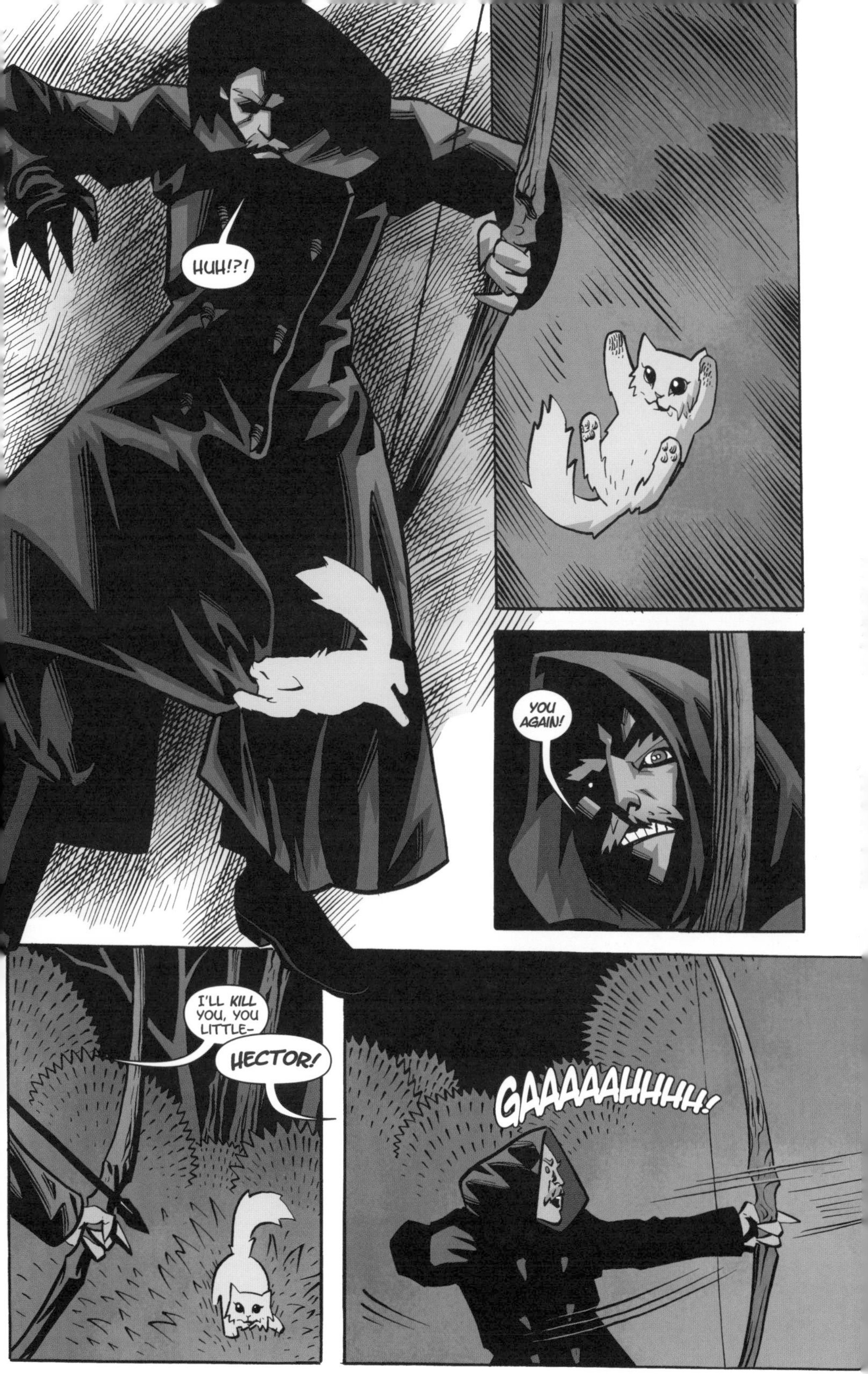
HUH!?!
YOU AGAIN!
I'LL KILL YOU, YOU LITTLE-
HECTOR!
GAAAAAHHHH!

EHEM.

PROFESSOR!?!

WHAT ARE YOU DOING HERE?

I MIGHT ASK YOU THE SAME QUESTION.

RATHER *UNSPORTSMANLIKE* CHOICE OF QUARRY, DON'T YOU THINK?

I'M SO SORRY, PROFESSOR. I WAS *HUNTING—*

I *KNOW* WHAT YOU WERE HUNTING.

I *THINK* YOU SHOULD GO HOME NOW.

BUT PROFESSOR...

YES, SIR.

AND YOU *TOO*, YOUNG LADY.

IT'S PAST YOUR BEDTIME.

WHEN COURTNEY RETURNED TO THE TREE, THE CATS HAD GATHERED AGAIN. BOO LAY IN A CORNER, LICKING MANY WOUNDS.

ARE YOU ALL *RIGHT?*

THE CLAW THAT DOES NOT SLAY ME STRENGTHENS ME.

DID YOU *CATCH* IT? THE *WILL-O-THINGY?*

NO.

MITTENS.

A *GREAT HUNTER.* BETTER THAN I.

HE TRACKED HIS *PREY* AS I *NEVER COULD.*

YET HE'S NOT AS WISE AS *SOME* AMONG US. HE *FORGOT,* OR NEVER *LEARNED,* THAT THE *ELVEN FIRE* LURES THOSE WHO SEEK IT TO THEIR *DOOM.*

MITTENS SANK INTO THE *MARL-PIT.*

A HUNTER MUST BE WISE IN THE WAYS OF HIS PREY.

I'LL NOT FORGET, TOBERMORY.

SO YOU STILL DON'T HAVE A LEADER.

OH, WE DO. THE WORTHIEST AMONG US.

CERTAINLY THE FASTEST.

AND PERHAPS THE WISEST.

QUICK LOOKED DOWN AT COURTNEY WITH A SATISFIED EXPRESSION.

IN HER PAWS, STILL STRUGGLING, WAS A CURIOUS CREATURE, SUCH AS COURTNEY HAD NEVER SEEN BEFORE.

OH BUGGER.

SURE GLAD IT'S SATURDAY.

"NOW I'M GONNA GET IT," SHE THOUGHT, IMAGINING THE HUNDRED DANGEROUS THINGS SHE DID THAT NIGHT.

COURTNEY. COME THIS WAY, PLEASE.

ARE YOU MAD AT ME?

NOT AT ALL.

RATHER IMPRESSED, ACTUALLY.

BUT THERE'S *SOMEONE* HERE WHO'D LIKE TO THANK YOU *PROPERLY* FOR YOUR BRAVERY LAST NIGHT.

WHAT ARE YOU *TALKING* ABOUT—

OH.

COURTNEY, THIS IS *SKARROW*.

HE'LL BE STAYING AS MY *GUEST* FOR A WHILE.

UH... HI.

# Chapter Three

MADAM HARKEN'S GARDEN WAS OVERGROWN EVEN BY HILLSBOROUGH STANDARDS, AND THAT'S SAYING SOMETHING.

BUT THEN, AS YOU MAY HAVE HEARD, SHE WASN'T THE SORT OF WITCH WHO STROVE TO KEEP UP APPEARANCES.

I CALLED YOU *ROUND* AS SOON AS I'D *HEARD*, PROFESSOR.

YOU KNOW HER BEST.

PERHAPS. YEARS AGO.

THE HOUSE WAS DARK AND DISHEVELED; BOOKS CLUTTERED THE SHELVES, KNICK-KNACKS OBSESSIVELY COLLECTED ON EVERY SURFACE.

DUST COATED EVERYTHING.

MADAM HARKEN?

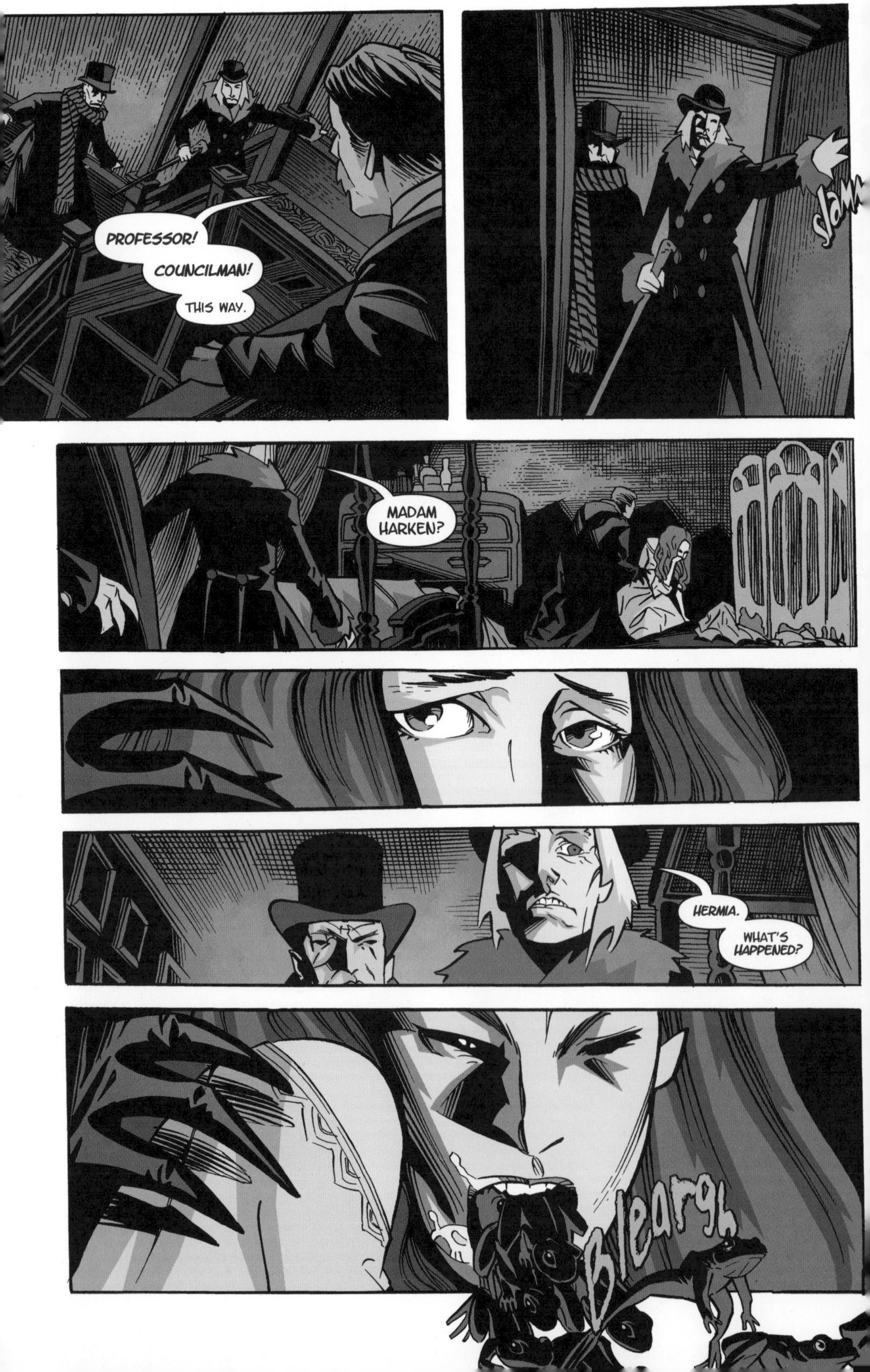
PROFESSOR!
COUNCILMAN!
THIS WAY.
slam
MADAM HARKEN?
HERMIA.
WHAT'S HAPPENED?
Bleargh

STRANGE.

SHE HAD SUCH *PROMISE.* A *GREAT FAMILY,* THE HARKENS.

HOW SHE CAME TO *THIS...*

WHAT *EXACTLY* DO YOU THINK *HAPPENED* HERE, WOODRUE?

IT'S *NOT* TOO HARD TO *GUESS.*

MADAM HERMIA'S LITTLE *"MINION"* TURNED ON HER AT *LAST.*

INEVITABLE, IF YOU ASK ME.

BUT *HECTOR* WILL TRACK IT DOWN.

I SERIOUSLY DOUBT THAT.

WHY?

BECAUSE I HAVE THE CREATURE UNDER MY PROTECTION.

YOU *WHAT!?!*

THE TWO WARLOCKS WERE INTERRUPTED BY THE SOUNDS OF COMMOTION FROM THE FRONT YARD.

OH DEAR.

WORD'S GOTTEN OUT.

LADIES AND *GENTLEMEN,* EVERYTHING IS IN *HAND* HERE.

PLEASE DON'T BE ALARMED.

WHERE'S MISS HARKEN!?!

WHAT'S HAPPENING?

WHAT ARE YOU GOING TO DO ABOUT IT!?

PLEASE, PEOPLE! LET US *THROUGH.*

IN TRUTH, NO WITCH OR WARLOCK HAD EVEN SEEN MADAM HARKEN IN YEARS, AND MOST HAD NEVER SEEN HER UP CLOSE.

GOOD HEAVENS, LOOK AT HER.

BREATHTAKING!

HASN'T AGED A DAY.

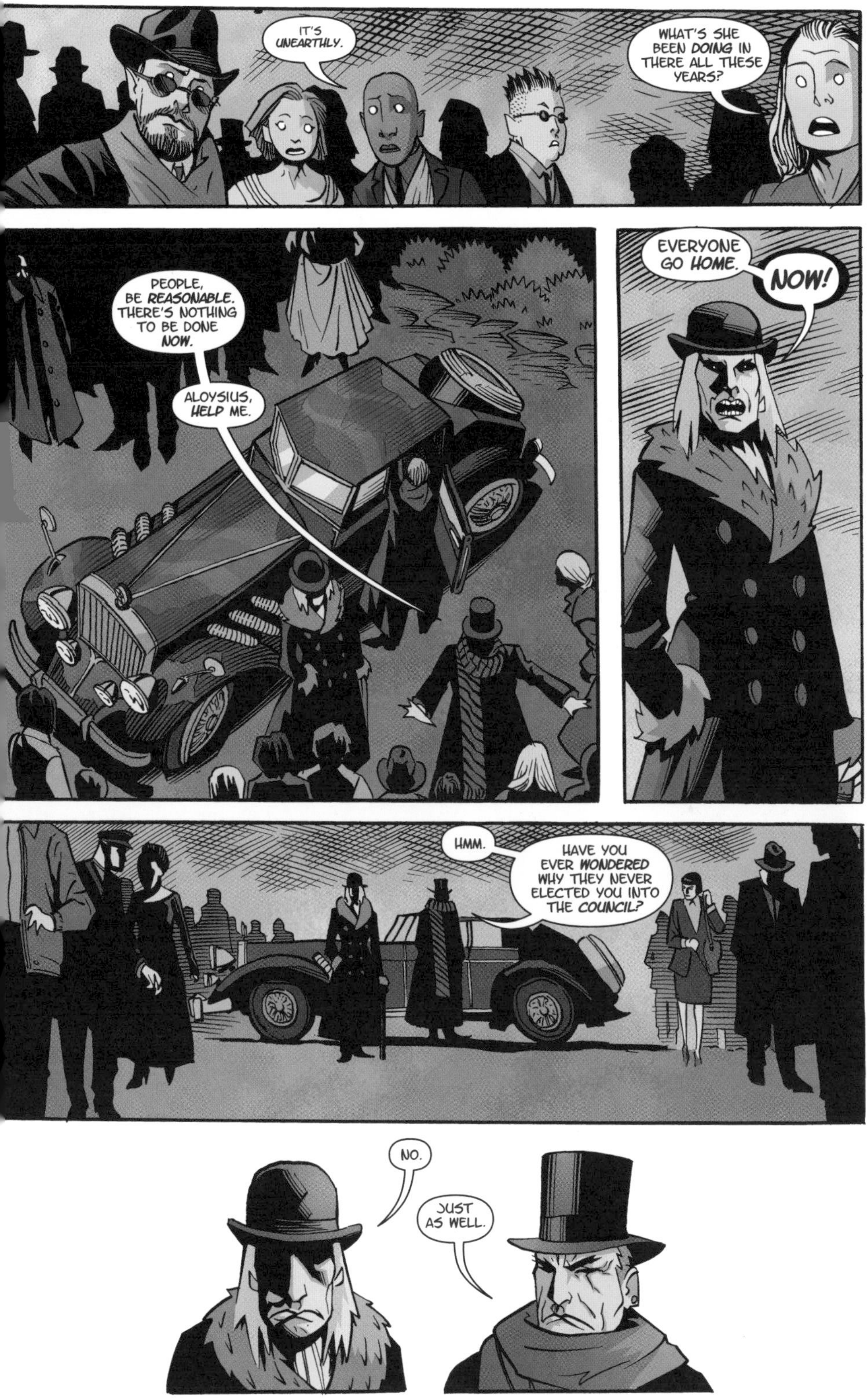

IT'S UNEARTHLY.
WHAT'S SHE BEEN DOING IN THERE ALL THESE YEARS?
PEOPLE, BE REASONABLE. THERE'S NOTHING TO BE DONE NOW.
ALOYSIUS, HELP ME.
EVERYONE GO HOME.
NOW!
HMM.
HAVE YOU EVER WONDERED WHY THEY NEVER ELECTED YOU INTO THE COUNCIL?
NO.
JUST AS WELL.

COURTNEY?

MMM, HUH?

OH, HEY, UNCLE A.

SORRY TO DISTURB YOU. I JUST WANTED TO SEE THAT YOU WERE ALL RIGHT.

YEAH. WE'RE COOL.

I ALWAYS WONDERED IF YOU HAD TEETH. GOOD TO KNOW.

HOW ABOUT SOME BREAKFAST?

IT'S WEIRD. IT'S LIKE I JUST KNOW WHAT HE MEANS.

HE DOESN'T HAVE TO SAY ANYTHING.

I KNOW.

WHY WERE THOSE *MEN* TRYING TO *KILL* HIM LAST NIGHT?

THEY BELIEVE HE *DID* SOMETHING...

...SOMETHING *EXTREMELY CRUEL,* TO A *WITCH.*

WHAT?

A *CURSE.*

DID HE?

WHAT DO *YOU* THINK?

NO WAY.

I DUNNO, HE'S... HE'S LIKE A BIG PUPPY.

HE'S TOO *SWEET* TO DO ANYTHING *MEAN* TO ANYBODY. YA *KNOW?*

I DO.

KROCK

WHAT WAS THAT?

STAY HERE.

NOW YOU PEOPLE STAY OUTSIDE. THIS IS COUNCIL BUSINESS.

HE THINKS HE CAN JUST DO WHAT HE LIKES!

WE'RE GOING TO SEE THAT MONSTER DEAD, YOU HEAR ME!

HE'S NOT GETTING AWAY WITH IT!

GENTLEMEN, PLEASE—

CAN I HELP YOU PEOPLE?

UH...

SEE HERE, CRUMRIN.

YOU'D BETTER DELIVER THAT BEAST OVER TO US.

HAD I?

OR THERE'LL BE TROUBLE IN THIS HOUSE, I CAN TELL YOU...

NOW, JOSEPH—

WILL THERE?

SEEMS TO ME YOU'RE ALL TRESPASSING.

HECTOR IS MY WITNESS. I'VE EVERY RIGHT TO REDUCE YOU ALL TO SOOT—

WHAT'S GOING ON?

COURTNEY! GO BACK UPSTAIRS. EVERYTHING'S FINE.

WHO ARE YOU GUYS?

WE'RE...

WE'RE...

WHAT THE DEVIL IS GOING ON HERE?

HECTOR, DID YOU LET THESE PEOPLE INSIDE?

I COULDN'T STOP THEM, SIR. THEY WANT AN EXPLANATION.

THAT'S RIGHT. WHO'S IN AUTHORITY HERE? THE COUNCIL, OR ALOYSIUS CRUMRIN?

ALRIGHT, FOLKS, YOU'VE MADE YOUR POINT.

GO HOME AND LET US HANDLE THIS.

THE CROWD BEGRUDGINGLY ALLOWED ITSELF TO BE USHERED OUT OF THE HOUSE. COURTNEY WATCHED THEM GO, HER OPINION OF WITCH SOCIETY DROPPING BY THE SECOND.

YOUNG LADY, THAT WAS A VERY FOOLISH THING TO DO.

STOPPED 'EM, DIDN'T IT?

I HAD MATTERS WELL IN HAND. YOU COULD HAVE BEEN SERIOUSLY HURT.

THEY MAY BE WITCHES, BUT THEY'RE STILL PEOPLE.

STUPID, SELF-ABSORBED, REACTIONARY PEOPLE.

GLAD TO SEE THAT YOU HOLD SUCH A *HIGH OPINION* OF OUR *PEERS.*

YOUR PEERS, WOODRUE.

ALOYSIUS, WE'RE *HERE* TO TAKE THIS CREATURE *PRISONER.*

ARE YOU GOING TO STAND IN THE WAY OF THE *COUNCIL?*

YOU'RE NOT THE COUNCIL, AND NEITHER IS *HECTOR.*

YOU'LL HAVE TO HOLD A *COUNCIL SESSION* AND *PROVE* YOUR CLAIM BEFORE I ALLOW YOU ANYWHERE *NEAR* HIM.

DAMN YOU AND YOUR *STIFF NECK,* CRUMRIN—

HE'S *RIGHT,* SIR.

*TECHNICALLY* THE CREATURE IS HIS *PROPERTY,* AND AS *LAWKEEPERS,* WE HAVE TO PROVE OUR *CLAIM* TO IT.

FOR GOODNESS' *SAKE,* ALOYSIUS, YOU *SAW* WHAT IT DID TO THAT *WOMAN.* SHE WAS YOUR *STUDENT.*

AREN'T YOU *OUTRAGED?* HAVE YOU NO *HEART?*

MY HEART'S WORKING *FINE,* AND SO IS MY *BRAIN.*

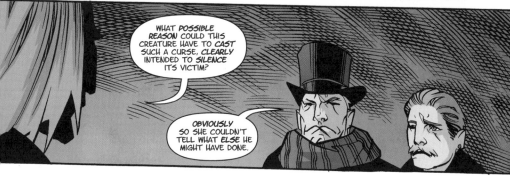

WHAT *POSSIBLE REASON* COULD THIS CREATURE HAVE TO *CAST* SUCH A CURSE, *CLEARLY* INTENDED TO *SILENCE* ITS VICTIM?

OBVIOUSLY SO SHE COULDN'T TELL WHAT *ELSE* HE MIGHT HAVE DONE.

AH, YES. HOW CLEVER.

THE *LIKELIEST* *SUSPECT* OF THE CRIME *COMMITTED* IT PRECISELY IN ORDER TO *SHIELD* HIMSELF FROM BLAME.

THAT *IS*, IF YOU CAN ASSEMBLE ENOUGH *NONSENSE* TO HOLD ONE.

NOW, *ALOYSIUS*, ARE YOU QUESTIONING OUR MARSHAL'S DETECTIVE WORK?

I *MIGHT*, WERE HE TO DO ANY.

I'LL SEE YOU TWO AT THE *COUNCIL* SESSION.

PLEASE DON'T *HESITATE* TO *GET OUT*.

COURTNEY?

YEAH?

K-KLAK

I *FORBID* YOU TO *INVOLVE* YOURSELF IN THIS MATTER.

I *MEAN* IT.

YES, SIR.

WHAT DO YOU KNOW ABOUT *SKARROW*?

THEY SAY 'E WERE ONCE A *MORTAL* CHILD TAKEN BY THE *KINDLY ONES* YEARS AGO.

TILL *YESTERDAY*, HE LIVED WITH OL' MADAM *HARKEN*, YONDER.

*HARKEN*. WHAT'S *HER* DEAL?

YOU SHOULD *KNOW*, MISSY. YOUR *UNCLE* TAUGHT HER.

ALWAYS ONE FOR STUDYIN' US *NIGHT THINGS*, MISS HARKEN.

CAUGHT ME IN THE *WOODS* COUPLE O' TIMES, WHEN SHE WERE A *LASS*. BUT SHE WERE *MUCH* NICER 'N *YOU*.

THINK I'D BETTER HAVE A *LOOK* AT HER.

GONNA BE HARD TE DO *THAT*. THEM *WARLOCKS* 'AVE 'ER UP AT *RADLEY HALL*.

NOBODY GETS IN *THERE* UNLESS THEY LET 'EM.

THAT *SO*?

A FIELD TRIP?

IT'S JUST THAT YOU'RE ALWAYS *SAYING* I NEED TO LEARN ABOUT *PRACTICAL* THINGS.

IF I'M GOING TO BE PART OF THIS, YA KNOW, *COVEN*, OR *WHATEVER*, I SHOULD KNOW SOMETHING *ABOUT* IT.

THAT'S *PRACTICAL*, ISN'T IT?

EXTREMELY SO.

TELL YOU *WHAT*. YOU *KNOW* THAT CREATIVE *WRITING* PROJECT YOU WERE PLANNING ON *NOT DOING*?

I WAS GOING TO—

UH HUH.

OKAY, I'LL DO IT.

AND *READ* IT IN FRONT OF *CLASS*, JUST LIKE EVERYONE *ELSE*.

YES, MS. CRISP.

RADLEY HALL WAS ONE OF THOSE BIG BLANK BUILDINGS WITH NO OBVIOUS SIGN OR LABEL, AND ONE NEVER SEES ANYONE ENTER OR LEAVE. IT WAS THE SORT OF BUILDING THAT ONE SIMPLY IGNORES, BECAUSE IT'S BEEN THERE SINCE BEFORE ANYONE CAN REMEMBER.

COURTNEY HAD PASSED THE PLACE EVERY DAY ON HER WALK TO SCHOOL, YET IT NEVER OCCURRED TO HER TO WONDER WHO USED IT, AND FOR WHAT PURPOSE.

MS. CRISP, AND MISS CRUMRIN.

JUST TAKING MY *STUDENT* ON A *TOUR*. WE WON'T *DISTURB* ANYONE. SHE WANTS TO SEE THE *HALL* OF *WONDERS.*

NAMES?

WHAT'S THE *HALL* OF *WONDERS?*

YOU'LL SEE.

CALPURNIA?

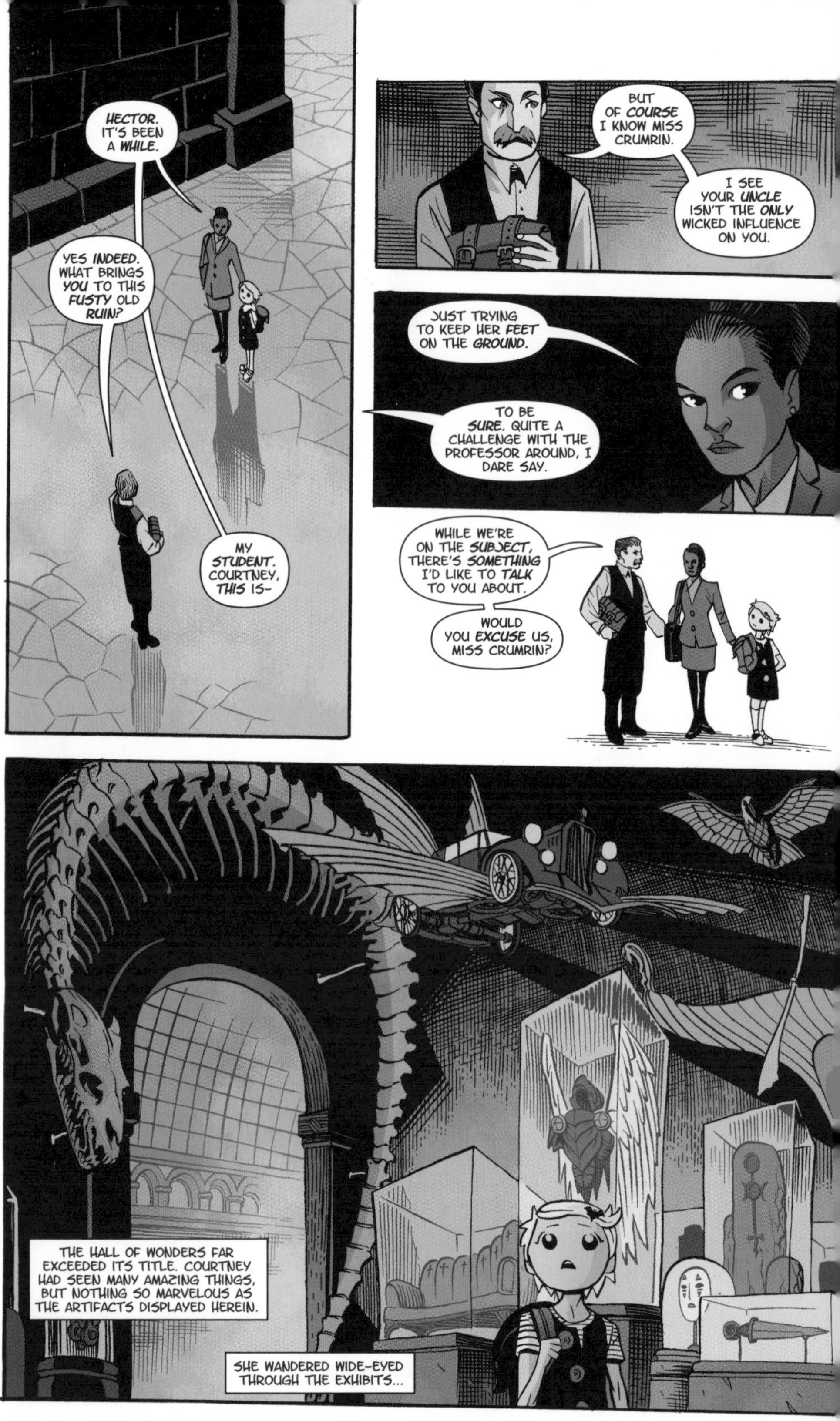
HECTOR. IT'S BEEN A WHILE.
YES INDEED. WHAT BRINGS YOU TO THIS FUSTY OLD RUIN?
MY STUDENT. COURTNEY, THIS IS-
BUT OF COURSE I KNOW MISS CRUMRIN.
I SEE YOUR UNCLE ISN'T THE ONLY WICKED INFLUENCE ON YOU.
JUST TRYING TO KEEP HER FEET ON THE GROUND.
TO BE SURE. QUITE A CHALLENGE WITH THE PROFESSOR AROUND, I DARE SAY.
WHILE WE'RE ON THE SUBJECT, THERE'S SOMETHING I'D LIKE TO TALK TO YOU ABOUT.
WOULD YOU EXCUSE US, MISS CRUMRIN?
THE HALL OF WONDERS FAR EXCEEDED ITS TITLE. COURTNEY HAD SEEN MANY AMAZING THINGS, BUT NOTHING SO MARVELOUS AS THE ARTIFACTS DISPLAYED HEREIN.
SHE WANDERED WIDE-EYED THROUGH THE EXHIBITS...

...UNTIL SHE CAME UPON AN UNPLEASANTLY FAMILIAR FACE.

RAWHEAD AND BLOODY BONES
~ Destroyed by the Council of Elders ~

YEAH *RIGHT*. DESTROYED BY *COMMITTEE*.

SUDDENLY, THOUGH SHE COULDN'T SAY WHY, COURTNEY KNEW SHE WAS BEING WATCHED.

YOU'VE GOOD *EYES* FOR A *MORTAL*.

I'VE *NEVER* BEEN SPOTTED *BEFORE*.

TOBERMORY?

I *THOUGHT* YOU SMELT FAMILIAR, THOUGH YOU'VE PUT ON SOME *WEIGHT* SINCE WE LAST MET.

AND *LOST* A BIT OF *FUR*. HOW DID YOU GET *IN*?

I HAVE MY METHODS. IT'S *BEST* TO KEEP AN EYE ON YOU MORTALS.

THERE YOU ARE.

PRETTY *AWFUL*, HUH?

THOUGH I GATHER THIS ISN'T YOUR *FIRST CLOSE LOOK.*

HMMM. WHAT'D THE *COP* WANT?

HECTOR? OH, *NOTHING IMPORTANT.*

WAS IT ABOUT MY *UNCLE?*

WHAT MAKES YOU THINK *THAT?*

I GOT MY *SOURCES.*

SO I'VE *GATHERED.*

YES, HE WANTED ME TO *TALK* WITH ALOYSIUS. AND I *WILL.*

WHAT ARE YOU GOING TO SAY?

JUST TO BE *CAREFUL* HOW HE HANDLES THE *COUNCIL.*

YOUR *UNCLE* HAS ALIENATED A *LOT* OF PEOPLE OVER THE YEARS.

THAT'S *NOT* ALWAYS SUCH A *WISE* WAY TO *LIVE.*

HE SEEMS TO DO OKAY. NOBODY *MESSES* WITH HIM.

*ISOLATION* ISN'T EVERYTHING.

IT'S NOT *WISE* TO TURN YOUR *BACK* ON THE *WORLD.*

COURTNEY DIDN'T CARE FOR MS. CRISP AT ALL, BUT SHE KNEW THAT HER TEACHER WAS NO FOOL. SHE WEIGHED THOSE LAST WORDS THOUGHTFULLY AS SHE WALKED HOME.

I DON'T HAVE ANY MORE MONEY.

BETTER GET YOUR *PARENTS* TO UP YOUR *ALLOWANCE*. YOU'RE GOING TO *NEED* IT.

"THE WORLD CAN BE A PRETTY SUCKY PLACE," THOUGHT COURTNEY. "SMALL WONDER UNCLE ALOYSIUS DOESN'T GET TOO INVOLVED IN IT."

WORKING ON THE CASE?

BRUSHING UP ON THE ARCHAIC *LAWS* REGARDING SKARROW'S *KIND.*

WARLOCKS HAVE *NEVER* TRUSTED THE NIGHT THINGS.

WHY NOT?

*WITCHCRAFT* CAME INTO BEING *PARTIALLY* TO *COUNTER* THE CREATURES OF THE UNDERWORLD.

IN *OLDEN* TIMES THEY WERE BLAMED FOR *EVERYTHING* FROM *ECLIPSES* TO *TOOTHACHES.*

I'M *AFRAID* THE PREJUDICE HAS *STUCK* THROUGHOUT THE *AGES,* DESPITE *CENTURIES* OF *RESEARCH.* PEOPLE LIKE *WOODRUE* WOULD STILL USE THEM AS *SCAPEGOATS* FOR ALL THE WORLD'S *SORROWS.*

BUT YOU WON'T LET THEM *HURT* HIM, *WILL* YOU?

I'LL *CERTAINLY* DO MY *BEST,* MY DEAR.

I'VE BEEN *THINKING.* SKARROW DIDN'T CAST THAT CURSE, *RIGHT?*

SO WHO *DID?*

GOOD QUESTION.

*UNFORTUNATELY,* THE ONLY PERSON WHO MIGHT *KNOW* CANNOT TELL US.

"WE'LL SEE ABOUT THAT," THOUGHT COURTNEY.

MISSY? THAT YOU?

YEAH. WHO'S THE *RUNT?*

ME LITTLE *BROTHER,* BUTTERBUG.

RUH!

WHAT'D YOU BRING *HIM* FOR? COULDN'T FIND A BABYSITTER?

TOUGH JOB, RADLEY HALL... *THOUGHT* YE COULD USE THE *HELP.*

SHOULDN'T BE *TOO* HARD. I HAVE AN INSIDE *MAN.*

THIS WAY.

*ISN'T* THERE A *HUGE,* SLAVERING MASTIFF THAT PROTECTS THE *GROUNDS*?

THERE *USED* TO BE.

I'VE BEEN KEEPING AN EYE ON THIS AFFAIR FOR *WEEKS*, EVER SINCE THE *HOBGOBLIN* EMERGED FROM ITS LONG *BANISHMENT*.

BREAK IN A *LOT*, DO YA?

SOMETHING AROUND HERE SMELLS EVEN *WORSE* THAN HE DID.

AS RAY OF MOONLIGHT PIERCES GLASS, SO SHALL TOBERMORY PASS.

TAKE *NOTE*, MISS CRUMRIN.

IT'S MUCH SIMPLER TO *TRICK* A SPELL THAN TO *BREAK* IT.

*WARLOCKS* ALWAYS DO IT THE *HARD* WAY.

THIS IS WHERE I LEAVE *YOU*. I'VE BUSINESS OF MY OWN.

COOL.

THANKS FOR THE HELP.

THIS MUST BE *HECTOR'S* OFFICE.

LOOKS LIKE AN *INCIDENT* REPORT FOR LAST *NIGHT*.

'R SOMETHING.

HMMM...

MADAM *HARKEN* MUST BE THROUGH *THERE*.

HERE, TAKE THIS PEN.

CAN YOU WRITE?

DO YOU SEE *THAT*, SIR?

DIABOLICAL.

NO, NOT HER. THERE'S SOMEONE ELSE I NEED TO TALK TO. *DOWNSTAIRS.*

THERE.

FER GOODNESS' SAKE, MISS. YE'VE GOT TE BE *JOKIN'!*

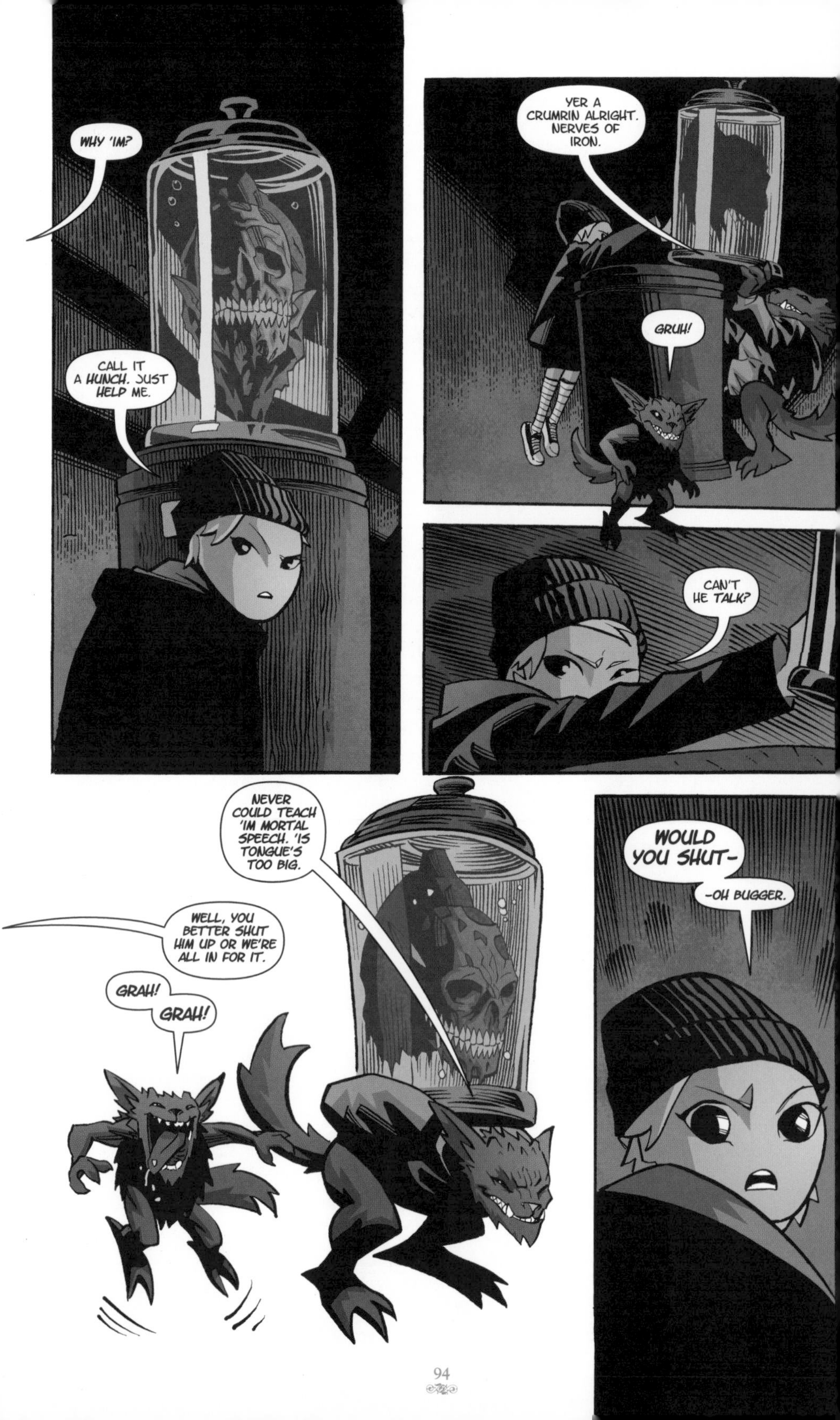
WHY 'IM?
CALL IT A HUNCH. JUST HELP ME.
YER A CRUMRIN ALRIGHT. NERVES OF IRON.
GRUH!
CAN'T HE TALK?
NEVER COULD TEACH 'IM MORTAL SPEECH. 'IS TONGUE'S TOO BIG.
WELL, YOU BETTER SHUT HIM UP OR WE'RE ALL IN FOR IT.
GRAH!
GRAH!
WOULD YOU SHUT-
-OH BUGGER.

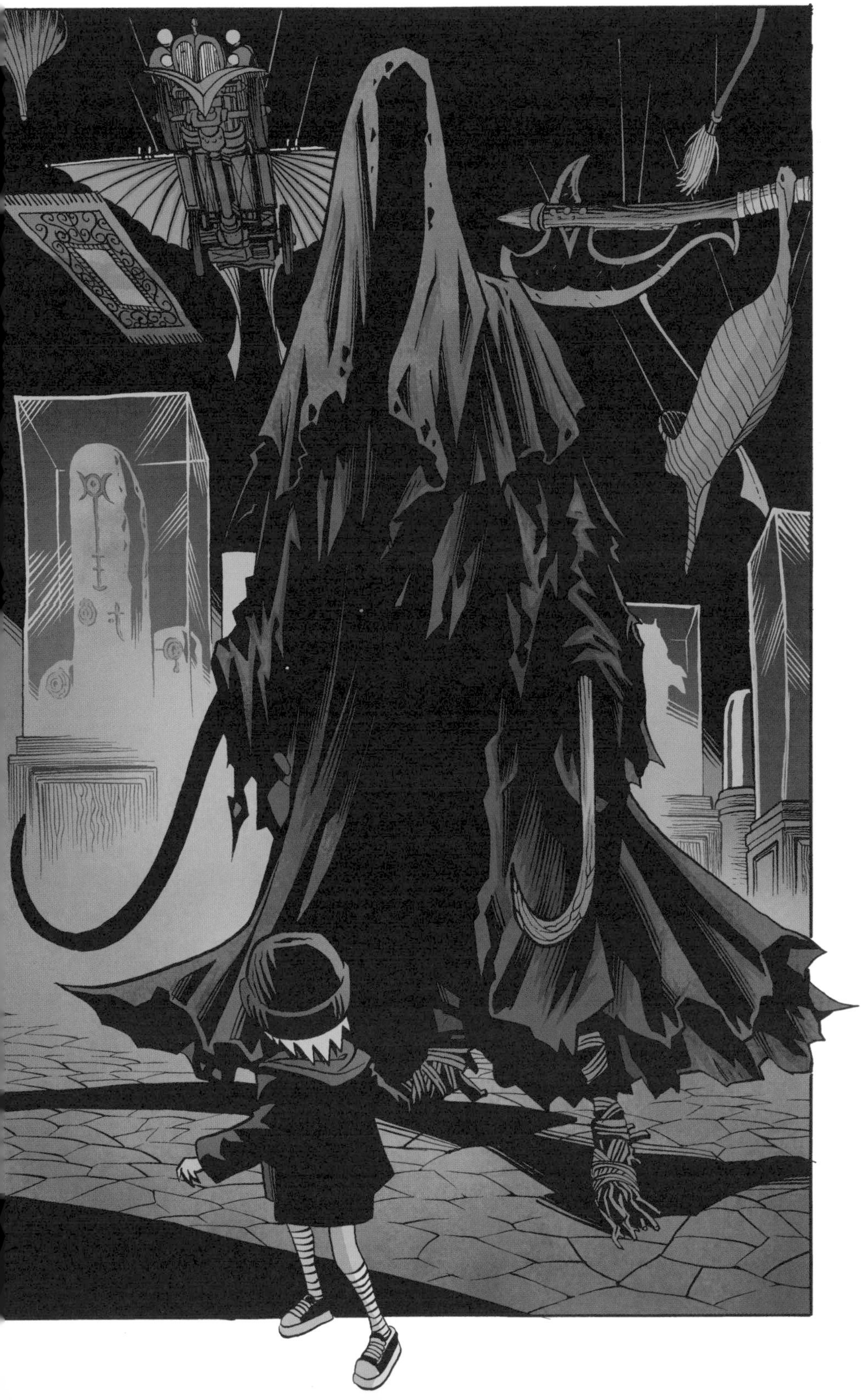

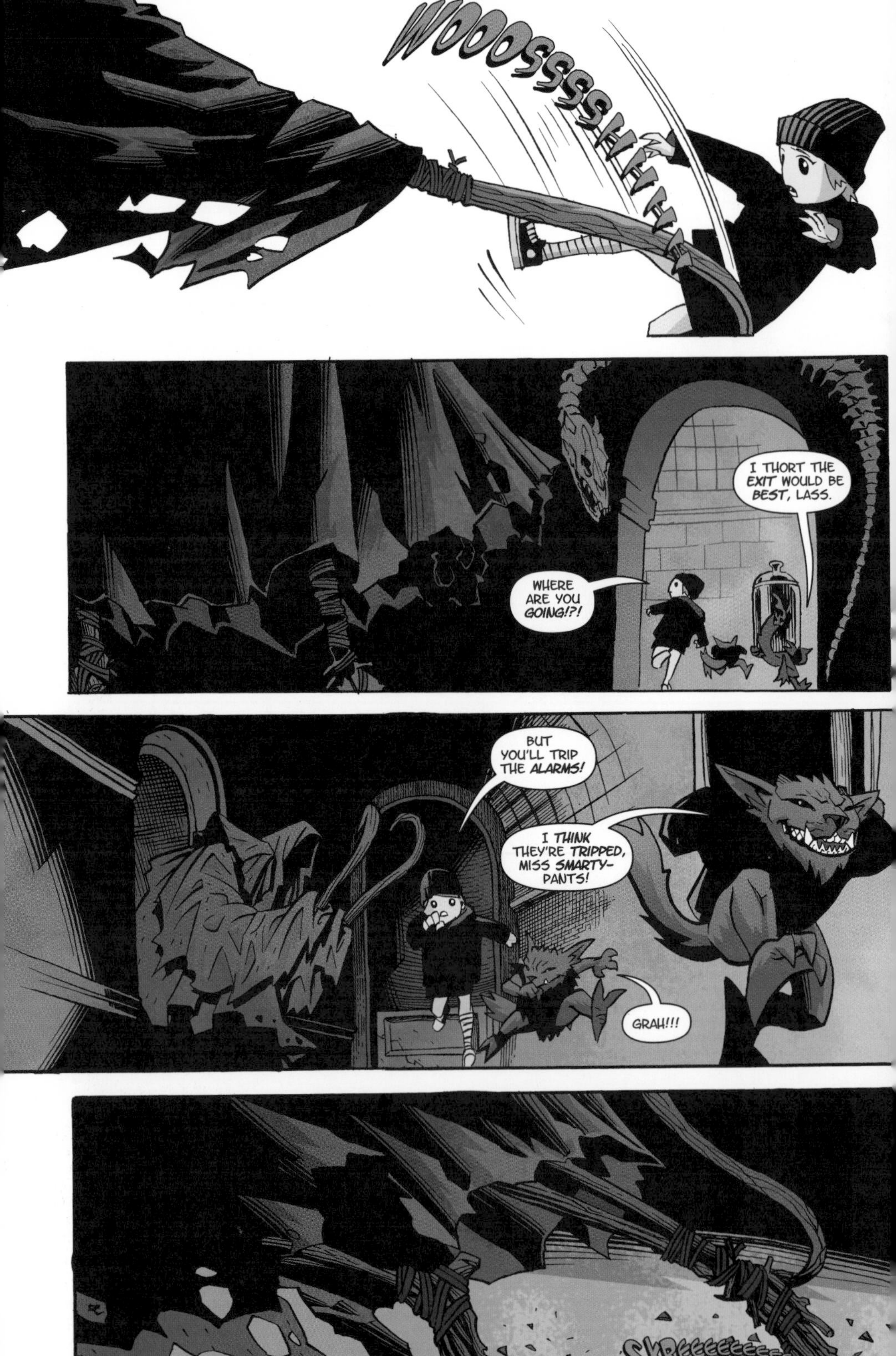
WOOOSSSSHHHH
I THORT THE EXIT WOULD BE BEST, LASS.
WHERE ARE YOU GOING!?!
BUT YOU'LL TRIP THE ALARMS!
I THINK THEY'RE TRIPPED, MISS SMARTY-PANTS!
GRAH!!!
SKREEEEEEEEEEE

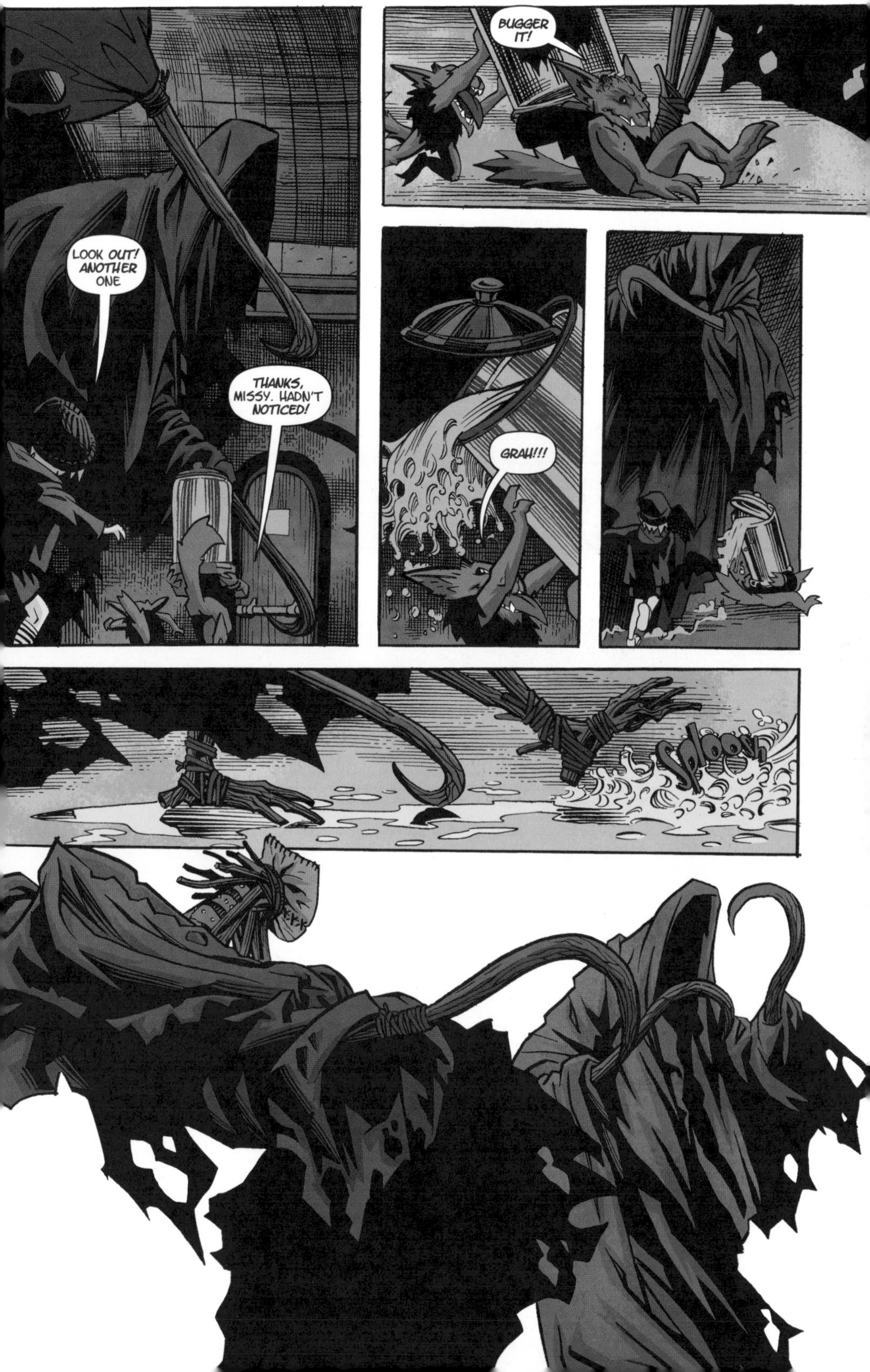
BUGGER IT!
LOOK OUT! ANOTHER ONE
THANKS, MISSY. HADN'T NOTICED!
GRAH!!!
SPLOOSH

KEEP DOOR
CLOSED AT
ALL TIMES

KEEP DOOR
CLOSED AT
ALL TIMES

Snap

# Chapter Four

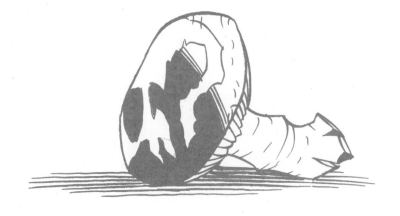

THE JAUNDICE ROOT, PLEASE.

SIX SHILLINGS.

OW, HEY!

A MORTAL!

A MORTAL!

MIND YOUR OWN BUSINESS, FUZZY!

ANYBODY ELSE WANT SOME O' THIS!?!

WHAT UNDER *EARTH* IS GOING ON?

THIS *MORTAL* ATTACKED ME, YOUR *DREADFULNESS*.

YOU BETTER *BELIEVE* IT, PAL. BACK OFF UNLESS YOU WANT ANOTHER ONE!

BRING HER TO ME.

*HAH!* SERVES YOU *RIGHT*, MORTAL. I'M AN *IMPORTANT GOBLIN* AROUND HERE.

COURTNEY CONSIDERED MAKING A RUN FOR IT, BUT THE APPROACHING CREATURE'S POWERFUL SINEWS AND SHARP CLAWS TESTIFIED TO THE FUTILITY OF THE IDEA.

MY UNCLE WON'T LIKE THIS.

HONESTLY, MY DEAR. SUCH CHILDISH THREATS ARE *BENEATH* YOU.

JAUNDICE ROOT.

BLACK BELLADONNA.

SALAMANDER BILE.

I KNOW ALOYSIUS CRUMRIN WELL ENOUGH TO *GUESS* THAT THIS ISN'T *HIS* SHOPPING LIST.

NECROMANCY ISN'T HIS STYLE.

A LITTLE HOBBY OF YOUR *OWN*?

WHAT'S IT TO YOU?

NOTHING. HUMAN AFFAIRS ARE ALL *ONE* TO ME.

SO LONG AS THEY DON'T INVOLVE MY PEOPLE.

YOU HAVEN'T HEARD ABOUT THE *TRIAL*, THEN?

ABOUT *SKARROW*?

I'VE *HEARD*, CHILD.

I'M TRYING TO HELP HIM.

SEE, A LOT OF WEIRD STUFF HAS BEEN HAPPENING.

IT DOESN'T TAKE A GENIUS TO GUESS THAT WHOEVER SUMMONED THAT MONSTER A FEW WEEKS AGO, THAT TOMMY THE BLOODY BONEHEAD, YA KNOW, PROBABLY DID THE CURSE ON THE WITCH-CHICK.

WHY DO YOU CARE WHAT HAPPENS TO A NIGHT THING?

I DON'T KNOW. 'CAUSE I LIKE HIM, I GUESS.

I FIGURE HE'S GOT SOME MAGICAL AURA, LIKE A GLAMOUR SPELL. I'M NOT STUPID, I'VE NOTICED. BUT EVEN SO, IT'S NOT FAIR TO BLAME HIM FOR OTHER PEOPLE'S CRAP.

I SEE.

HE'S ONE OF YOUR PEOPLE, ISN'T HE? YOU'RE A BIG SHOT DOWN HERE. CAN'T YOU HELP?

HE'S MORE THAN MY PEOPLE, HE'S MY CHILD.

WHAT!?!

CENTURIES AGO, HE WAS A HUMAN BOY.

I TOOK HIM AS MY OWN, AND LEFT A CHANGELING IN HIS PLACE.

BUT AT LAST HE YEARNED FOR THE HUMAN WORLD AND LEFT ME.

HUH! WHAT THE HECK WOULD HE DO THAT FOR?

I DO NOT KNOW.

HE ONCE TOLD ME THAT HE SOUGHT IN *HUMAN* AFFECTION A WARMTH WHICH *MY* PEOPLE DON'T *POSSESS.*

I'VE NOT SEEN HIM IN MANY YEARS.

BUT HE'S STILL YOUR SON. YOU CAN *HELP* HIM.

NO. WHEN HE LEFT THE *UNDERWORLD,* HE *PUT* HIMSELF BEYOND MY *AID.*

I WILL NOT INTERFERE.

YEAH, I GET IT. AND YOU *REALLY* DON'T *UNDERSTAND* WHY HE LEFT?

I WILL DO *SOMETHING* FOR HIM.

I WILL LET *YOU* RETURN TO THE *WORLD* ABOVE.

I HAVE NO *ILLUSIONS* ABOUT HIS CHANCES WITH YOUR FELLOW *MORTALS...*

BUT PERHAPS YOUR COMPANY WILL MAKE HIS LAST DAYS *SWEETER.*

YEAH. THANKS A *BUNCH.*

OH, AND *MORTAL?*

YEAH?

IF HE HAS ANY *GLAMOUR,* IT IS A KIND NATURAL TO *YOUR* FOLK, NOT *MINE.*

"PERHAPS", THOUGHT COURTNEY, "IT WAS TRUE THAT HUMANS WERE MORE CAPABLE OF LOVE AND AFFECTION." THINGS THAT COURTNEY HAD KNOWN LITTLE OF UNTIL RECENTLY.

BUT THEY WERE CERTAINLY MORE CAPABLE OF CRUELTY AND VIOLENCE, AT LEAST, SO FAR AS SHE'D SEEN. EVEN THE WORST NIGHT THING SHE'D EVER MET WAS DRIVEN TO KILL BY SOME HUMAN MONSTER.

YOU *BLEW* IT, LEAVING *YOUR* PEOPLE TO BE WITH *US.*

WHAT'S *HERMIA HARKEN* EVER DONE FOR *YOU?*

SHE *LOVED* YOU, *DIDN'T SHE?*

COURTNEY UNDERSTOOD SKARROW'S SILENCE BETTER THAN ANY WORDS.

"THERE WAS SOMETHING ABOUT BEING CARED FOR," SHE THOUGHT. SOMETHING MAGICAL.

Creative writing: Just because it happened to you doesn't make it interesting!

"SKARROW"...

BY...

UM ...COURTNEY CRUMRIN.

GO AHEAD, COURTNEY.

>SNORT<

HIS SWEETNESS SHINES LIKE A LIGHT...

FROM EYES OF BLACKEST...

...NIGHT.

>TITTER<

>SHHH<

AND WITHOUT A SINGLE WORD...

HE SAYS..

UM... HE SAYS... THE NICEST THINGS I'VE...

...EVER...

...HEARD.

DIMLY, AS COURTNEY READ AND THE HOTNESS OF EMBARRASSMENT FLUSHED HER FACE, SHE THOUGHT SHE COULD HEAR A THUNDERCLAP.

BUT PEOPLE *FEAR* AN OPEN *HEART.*

THE ROOM SEEMED TO DARKEN.

AND TEAR INNOCENCE APART.

HE'S CALLED A *MONSTER* BY THE FOOLS...

A DULL SENSE OF TOTAL HUMILIATION RESTED FIRMLY ON HER CHEST, MAKING BREATHING DIFFICULT, BUT SHE PLUNGED ON.

ROLLING THUNDER SHOOK THE ROOM, AND THE CHAIRS BEGAN TO VIBRATE.

WHO *TREAT* HIS KIND LIKE *PETS* AND *TOOLS.*

spak

COURTNEY BARELY NOTICED, HER ONE THOUGHT TO GET THROUGH HER STUPID POEM AND BE DONE WITH IT.

I WISH I KNEW THE PERFECT *CHARM*...

TO SAVE HIM FROM THOSE WHO MEAN HIM *HARM.*

Creati
because i
t mak

Courtney's Journal

MY GOODNESS. THAT WAS... POWERFUL STUFF, COURTNEY.

GOOD JOB.

PHEW.

WOW. THAT WAS A... REALLY COOL...

...POEM.

UH, THANKS.

DO YOU WANT TO WALK *HOME* WITH ME?

WHY?

WELL, CAUSE, LIKE, YOU'RE PRETTY COOL, AND... UM...

YOU KNOW THOSE *GUYS* THAT HANG OUT BY THE PLAYGROUND?

THEY'RE SCARED OF YOU, *RIGHT?*

YEAH, THEY ARE.

SO *NOW,* AFTER *IGNORING* ME ALL LAST YEAR, YOU'RE SUDDENLY MY *BUDDY?*

I GOT MORE *IMPORTANT* THINGS TO WORRY ABOUT THAN YOUR FIFTY-DOLLAR-A-DAY ALLOWANCE.

*FINE!* BE THAT WAY.

JERK.

O, DREADFUL SPIRIT, HEED MY CALL BY ELDRITCH POWER I THEE ENTHRALL.

SPEAK YE NOW THROUGH LIPS CLAY COLD DIVULGE THY SECRETS YET UNTOLD.

GOTCHA!

HA HA HA! I LOVE DOING THAT!

AH GOODNESS...

VERY FUNNY.

WHAT HAPPENED TO MY BODY?

UNCLE A, YOU KNOW, THE WARLOCK WHO KICKED YOUR ASS...

SO WHO SUMMONED YOU?

HE SAID THEY BURNED IT AND THREW THE ASHES INTO THE MARL-PIT.

OH WELL. I'VE HAD WORSE.

I CANNOT TELL, I'VE BEEN BOUND TO SILENCE.

WASTE OF TIME.

POOR GIRL. WISH I COULD HELP.

PERHAPS YOU SHOULD LOOK TO SEE WHO HAD THE MOST TO GAIN FROM MY MISCHIEF.

YOU JUST SAID YOU'RE UNDER A SILENCING SPELL.

WAIT A MINUTE!

DON'T HELPFUL HINTS COUNT?

YES, WELL.

THAT SORT OF SPELL IS TRICKY. THERE'S ALWAYS A LOOPHOLE.

AHEM... UNLESS THE VICTIM DOESN'T WANT TO TALK.

...IF YOU FOLLOW ME.

HMM. I THINK I DO...

WHEN THE COVEN OF MYSTICS HELD COUNCIL, NOT ALL MEMBERS OF THE COVEN WERE EXPECTED TO APPEAR, BUT MOST DID THAT DAY.

MS. CRISP TOLD COURTNEY THAT THEY NEEDED REASSURANCE THAT THE COUNCIL WAS STILL IN AUTHORITY, AND THAT ALOYSIUS CRUMRIN WAS STILL ANSWERABLE TO THEM.

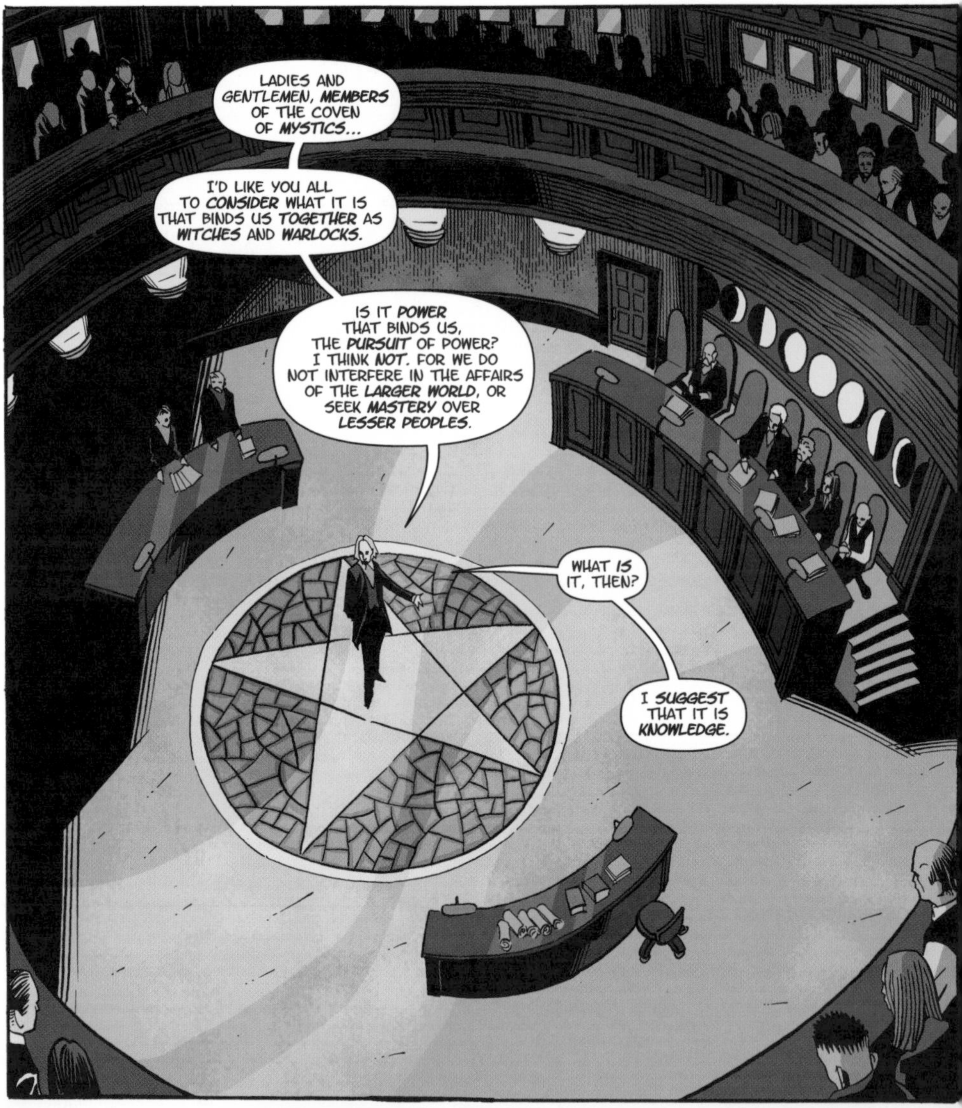
LADIES AND GENTLEMEN, MEMBERS OF THE COVEN OF MYSTICS...
I'D LIKE YOU ALL TO CONSIDER WHAT IT IS THAT BINDS US TOGETHER AS WITCHES AND WARLOCKS.
IS IT POWER THAT BINDS US, THE PURSUIT OF POWER? I THINK NOT. FOR WE DO NOT INTERFERE IN THE AFFAIRS OF THE LARGER WORLD, OR SEEK MASTERY OVER LESSER PEOPLES.
WHAT IS IT, THEN?
I SUGGEST THAT IT IS KNOWLEDGE.

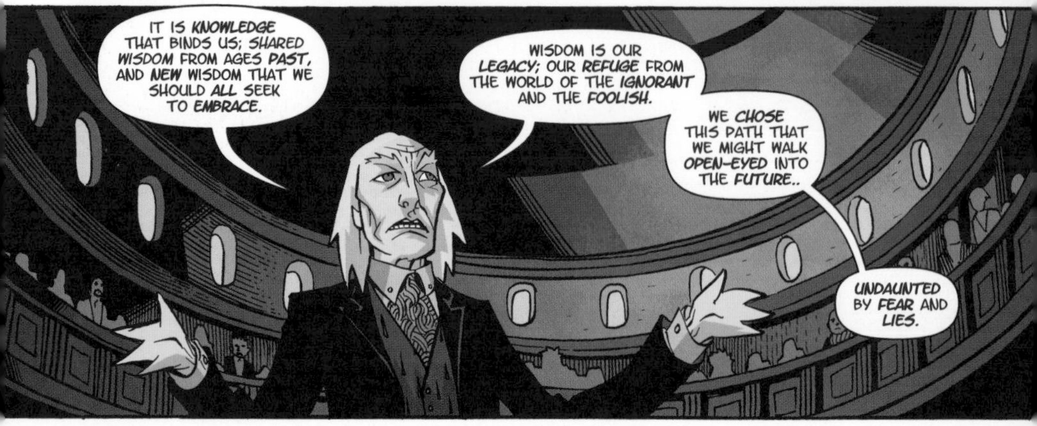
IT IS KNOWLEDGE THAT BINDS US; SHARED WISDOM FROM AGES PAST, AND NEW WISDOM THAT WE SHOULD ALL SEEK TO EMBRACE.
WISDOM IS OUR LEGACY; OUR REFUGE FROM THE WORLD OF THE IGNORANT AND THE FOOLISH.
WE CHOSE THIS PATH THAT WE MIGHT WALK OPEN-EYED INTO THE FUTURE..
UNDAUNTED BY FEAR AND LIES.

THE *CURSE* THAT HAS AFFLICTED ONE OF OUR NUMBER IS *NO CREATION* OF *ANY SIMPLE CREATURE* OF THE *UNDERWORLD*.

AND YET, SOME OF US *STILL* ARE *BESET* BY LIES, HANDED *DOWN* FROM *OLDEN* TIMES.

THE LIE PASSED DOWN THE *GENERATIONS* IS *NO LESS UNTRUE* THAN ANY *OTHER* SORT, THOUGH IT MAY BE HARDER TO *DISCOVER*. BUT IT IS OUR VERY *PURPOSE* TO *DISPEL* LIES, AND FIND THE *TRUTH*.

IT IS *COMPLEX* AND *SUBTLE*, DESIGNED FOR THE PURPOSE OF CONCEALING THE *TRUTH* AND *PERPETUATING* LIES.

DO NOT BE *FOOLED*, FOR ITS VERY *NATURE REVEALS* IT.

THE *NIGHT THINGS* ARE *NOT* CREATURES OF *DECEIT*. THAT IS THE REALM OF *MEN*.

JOHN MILTON MANDRAKE COUNCIL MEMBER 1278 - 2002

CHARLES LONDON COUNCIL MEMBER 1262 - 2002

THE *DARKNESS* THAT WE SEEK TO KEEP AT BAY DOES *NOT* COME FROM THE *UNDERWORLD*. IT IS *OUR* DARKNESS, FROM WITHIN OUR *OWN HEARTS*.

THE *SLAYING* OF A *SCAPEGOAT* WILL *NOT STOP* IT. THAT PATH WILL ONLY FEED THE *LIES*.

MANDRAKE...

THANK YOU, PROFESSOR.

MARSHALL *HUGHES*, YOU MAY *PROCEED* WITH YOUR OPENING STATEMENT.

I *THINK* I'VE FIGURED IT *OUT*, THE *CURSE*.

YOU KNOW THOSE TWO *COUNCIL GUYS* THAT DIED?

WELL, WHO *BENEFITS*?

AND WHO'S BEEN *HOVERING* OVER HERMIA HARKEN SINCE SHE WAS FOUND?

IT'S *WRATHUM*, YOU KNOW, THE *HEAD DUDE*, 'CAUSE—

DON'T BE *RIDICULOUS*.

CONSIDERING HE APPOINTED *BOTH* THOSE COUNCIL MEMBERS, WOODRUE *WRATHUM* IS THE *LEAST* LIKELY SUSPECT.

HE'S PRAYING THE REST OF THE COUNCIL ACCEPTS HIS *NEW* APPOINTMENT. IF *NOT*, HE LOSES THE *MAJORITY* AND *STOCKBROOK* WILL BE VOTED COUNCIL HEAD.

BUT *WHO* WILL HE...?

THANK YOU, COUNCILMAN WRATHUM.

I'D LIKE TO *BEGIN* BY EXPRESSING MY *UTMOST* RESPECT FOR THE ESTEEMED PROFESSOR *CRUMRIN*. I DEEPLY REGRET THAT THESE MATTERS HAVE CAUSED HIM SO MUCH *PERSONAL* TURMOIL.

SUDDENLY, ALL BECAME SICKENINGLY CLEAR.

AND HECTOR'S GENTLE, TROUBLED EXPRESSION SEEMED SUDDENLY MASKLIKE, DISGUISING THE TWISTED SCHEMES BENEATH.

SURELY, HE WOULD BE COUNCILMAN WRATHUM'S NEW APPOINTMENT.

THE SESSION WENT ON FOR SEVERAL MORE HOURS.

ALOYSIUS PRESENTED HIS DETAILED KNOWLEDGE OF NIGHT THINGS, POINTED OUT THE LONG COMPANION-SHIP BETWEEN MADAM HARKEN AND SKARROW, WHICH HE'D SEEN FIRSTHAND. HE POINTED OUT HOW VAGUE THE EVIDENCE WAS FOR THE CREATURE'S GUILT, HOW THIN AND UNLIKELY ITS MOTIVATIONS.

HECTOR POINTED OUT HOW UNPLEASANT THE MATTER WAS, AND HOW RELIEVING IT WILL BE TO PUT IT BEHIND THEM ALL.

THE COUNCIL DELIBERATED FOR LESS THAN AN HOUR.

PROFESSOR, WE *APPRECIATE* YOUR *EFFORTS*, BUT I'M *AFRAID* WE FEEL YOU'VE LOST YOUR *OBJECTIVITY* IN THIS MATTER.

THE COUNCIL HAS AGREED *UNANIMOUSLY* THAT FOR THE *SAFETY* OF OUR *COMMUNITY*, YOU MUST *RELINQUISH* YOUR PRISONER TO *US*.

YES, COUNCILMAN.

THEY CAN'T—

COURTNEY, ALOYSIUS CAN'T STAND *ALONE* AGAINST THE WHOLE *COVEN*.

THEY'RE GOING TO *KILL* HIM! HE DIDN'T DO ANYTHING!

DON'T YOU *SEE*? THEY ALL *KNOW* THAT.

IT DOESN'T *MATTER* WHO CAST THE CURSE, WHAT *MATTERS* IS THAT THEY HAVE AN *EXCUSE* TO *PUNISH* YOUR FRIEND *SKARROW* FOR STEALING MADAM *HARKEN* AWAY, AND TO PUNISH *HERMIA* FOR CHOOSING A *NIGHT THING* OVER THE *COVEN*.

WHAT!?!

IT'S ONE THING FOR A MAN LIKE YOUR *UNCLE* TO WITHDRAW INTO SOLITUDE, BUT A WOMAN LIKE *HERMIA*— UNFORGIVABLE.

WHY?

FOR *STARTERS*, HERMIA BELONGED TO AN *IMPORTANT* FAMILY.

HER *FATHER* WAS THE HEAD OF THE *COUNCIL* BEFORE *WRATHUM*. HE'D PROMISED HER TO *MARRY*...

WELL IT'S *TOO* LONG A *STORY*.

SHE SIMPLY DIDN'T *WANT* THE LIFE *CHOSEN* FOR HER, SO SHE *WALKED* AWAY.

BUT SKARROW! WE CAN'T DO ANYTHING?

ALOYSIUS THOUGHT THEY'D LISTEN TO HIM.

HE ASSUMED THAT HE COULD SIMPLY APPEAR AND EXPLAIN IT ALL, AND THEY'D UNDERSTAND.

HE MISCALCULATED.

WELL I'M NOT GOING TO JUST SIT HERE.

COURTNEY!

TAKING THE ROAD, IT WAS A FIFTEEN-MINUTE WALK TO CRUMRIN HOUSE. COURTNEY MADE IT THERE IN FIVE.

YOU'VE GOT TO GO.

NOW!

JUST RUN!
GO HOME!

THEY WON'T FIND YOU THERE.

AS SKARROW CREPT SLOWLY AWAY TOWARD A DARK OPENING INTO THE EARTH, COURTNEY WONDERED HOW MUCH HE TRULY UNDERSTOOD OF HIS DANGER.

A FIGURE, JUST VISIBLE IN THE GLOOM, WAITED. COURTNEY COULD GUESS, OR HOPE, WHO IT MIGHT BE.

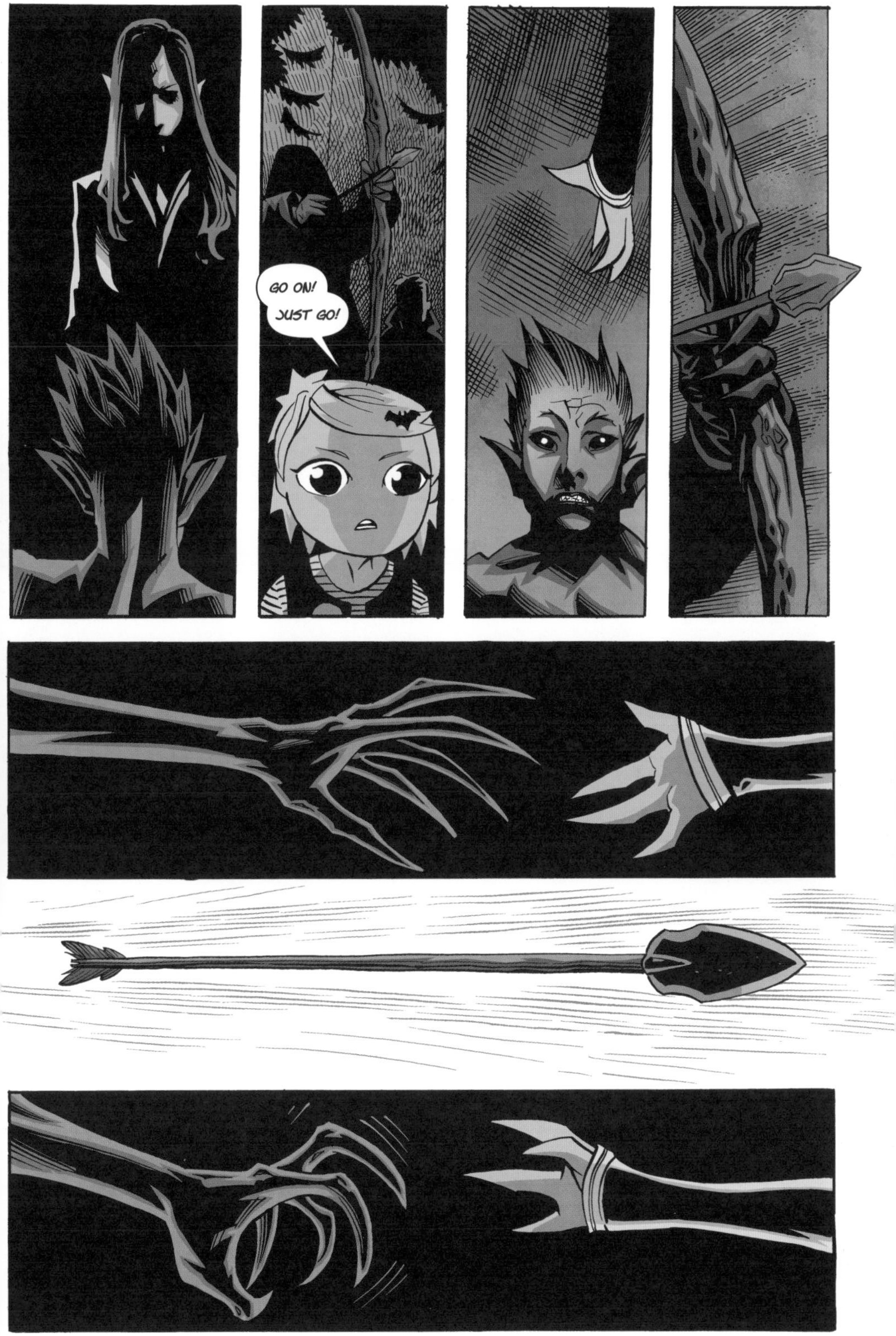
GO ON!
JUST GO!

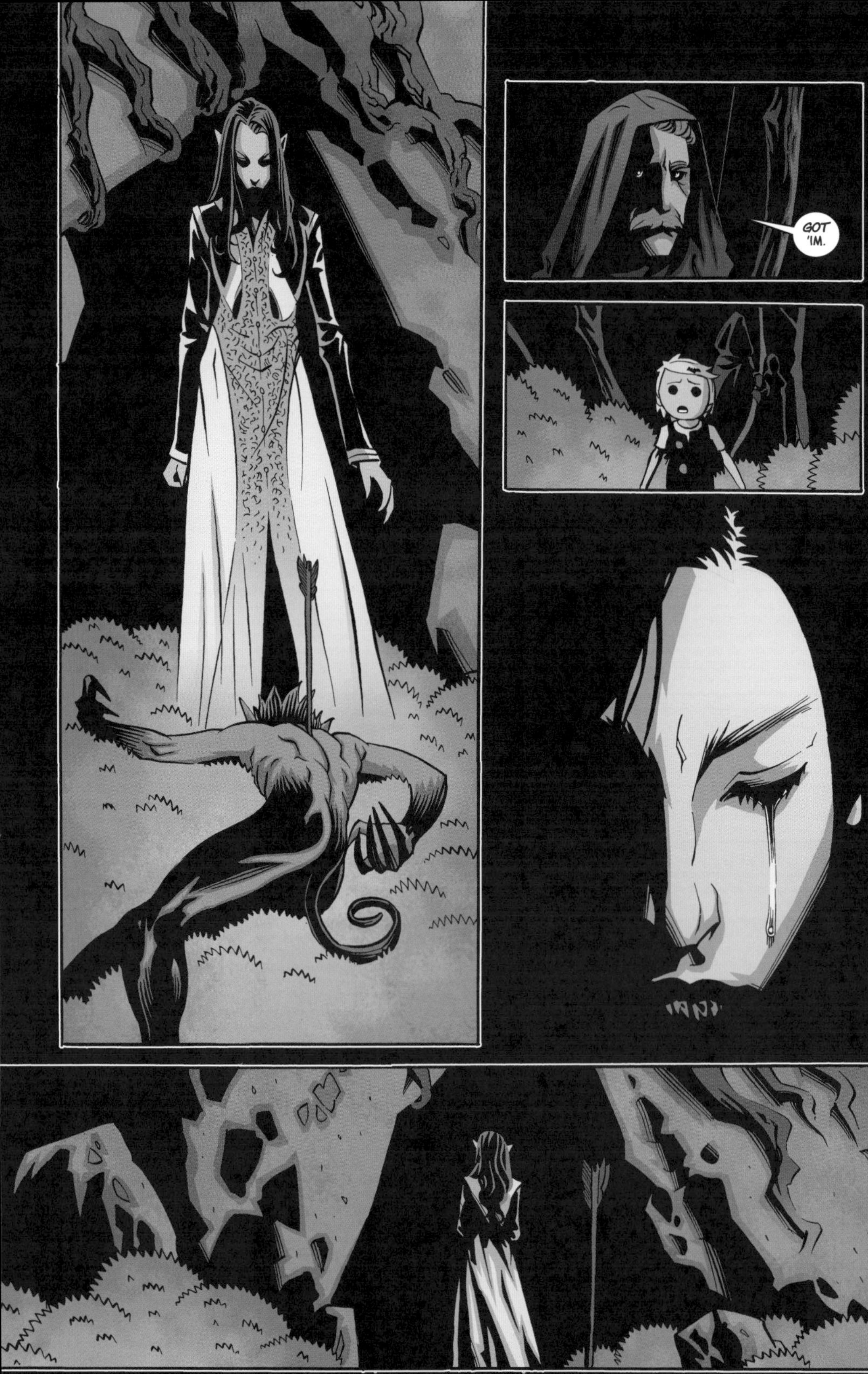
GOT 'IM.

A SAD WAY FOR THIS AFFAIR TO END.

WHY? YOU WANTED BLOOD, AND YOU GOT IT.

I HOPE TO HEAVEN YOU'RE SATISFIED.

THEY KILLED HIM!

THEY KILLED HIM!

THERE THERE, YOUNG LADY―

WOODRUE!! DON'T YOU DARE SPEAK TO MY NIECE!

I HATE YOU! I HATE YOU BOTH!! HOW COULD YOU LET THIS HAPPEN!?!

I CAN ASSURE YOU―

WOODRUE.

GET OUT NOW, OR SO HELP ME....

YOU COULD HAVE DONE SOMETHING. ANYTHING!

HOW? YOU'D LET HIM GO BEFORE I EVEN GOT HERE.

BUT–

COURTNEY, PLEASE!

LEAVE ME ALONE.

KRASSHHH.

A FEW DAYS LATER, IT WAS ANNOUNCED THAT THE CURSE WAS BROKEN.

THE FIRST THING MADAM HARKEN SAID WAS "YES," TO MARSHAL HECTOR HUGHES' PROPOSAL OF MARRIAGE.

COURTNEY LOOKED INTO HER EYES AND SAW A DEFEATED WOMAN.

LET'S GO BEFORE I PUKE.

IT'S NOT FAIR. SHE DIDN'T DO ANYTHING, SHE JUST DIDN'T WANT TO BE IN THEIR STUPID COVEN.

SHE TURNED HER BACK ON THE WORLD, JUST LIKE YOUR UNCLE. WHEN YOU DO THAT...

YOU CAN GET BITTEN ON THE ASS.

EXACTLY. WELL PUT.

COURTNEY WAS BEGINNING TO FIND MS. CRISP SOMEWHAT LESS AGGRAVATING LATELY, AND TALKING TO HER WAS ODDLY COMFORTING.

YOU SHOULD FORGIVE YOUR UNCLE, THOUGH.

HE LOVES YOU, AND THAT OUGHT TO COUNT FOR SOMETHING.

IT DOES.

"PERHAPS SHE HAS A POINT," THOUGHT COURTNEY. "IT IS UNWISE TO TURN YOUR BACK ON THE WORLD."

BUT IT'S DEADLY TO TURN YOUR BACK ON A CRUMRIN.

HERMIA?

HERE I AM.

I MUST SAY, THIS IS ALL RATHER MYSTERIOUS. WHY THIS PLACE?

YOUR NOTE SAID TO MEET HERE. IS THIS YOUR ATTEMPT AT ROMANCE, HECTOR? IF SO, IT'S IN POOR TASTE.

MY NOTE?

BUT I WROTE NO NOTE.

I WROTE YOU BOTH.

WASN'T SURE IT'D *WORK*, BUT YOU *COVEN* PEOPLE ARE *NOTHING* IF NOT *GULLIBLE*.

YOUNG *LADY*, IF *THIS* IS YOUR IDEA OF A *JOKE*—

*NO*, YOU'RE THE *JOKE!*

ALL THIS *PLANNING*, ALL THE *LIES* AND *MURDERS*, *JUST* SO YOU COULD BE TOP OF THE *HEAP*.

*CONGRATS*. BET YOU HARDLY *NOTICED* IT WAS A HEAP OF *DOG CRAP*.

THAT'S *NO WAY* TO TALK TO—

*SHUT UP!*

I'M *SICK* OF YOUR *BULL*.

YOU FED IT TO *WOODRUE* AND THE REST OF 'EM, AND THEY WERE SO *GRATEFUL* THEY *FOLLOWED* YOU LIKE *TRAINED MONKEYS*.

BUT NOT *RIGHT NOW.*

*RIGHT NOW* IT'S *JUST* YOU AND ME.

AND *WHAT* CAN *YOU* DO, *LITTLE GIRL?*

*ME?* NOT *MUCH*. I'M JUST A *KID*.

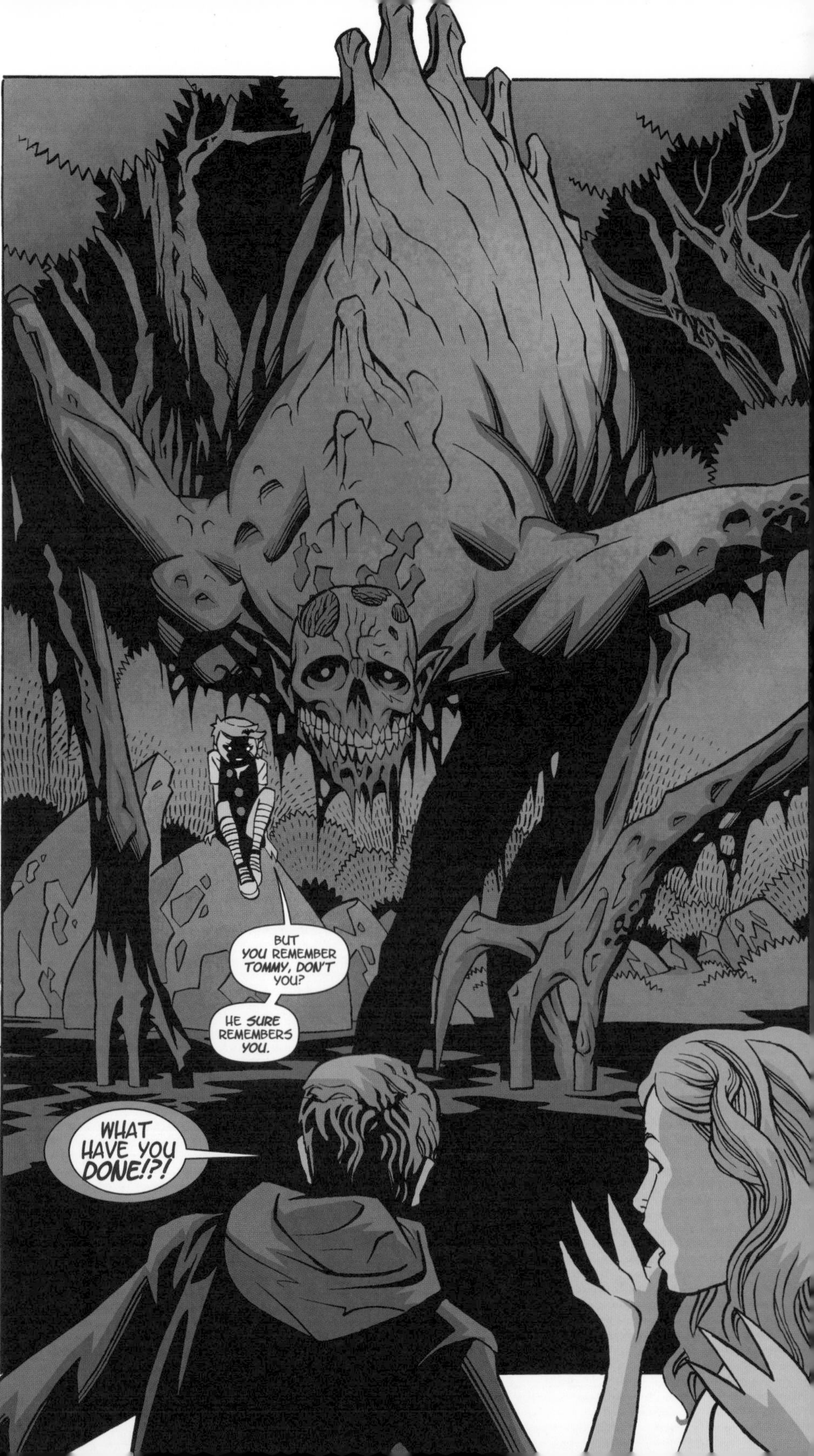
BUT YOU REMEMBER TOMMY, DON'T YOU?
HE SURE REMEMBERS YOU.
WHAT HAVE YOU DONE!?!

I DID THE SAME THING YOU DID.

I SUMMONED A MONSTER TO DO MY DIRTY WORK.

COME ALONG NOW, LITTLE HECTOR.

DOWN TO THE BOTTOM YOU GO.

WITH ALL THE OTHER CHILDREN WHO TELL LIES AND SPEAK PROFANE CURSES.

HERMIA, HELP ME!

SAVE YOUR BREATH.

SHE CAN'T HELP ANYONE, NOT EVEN HERSELF.

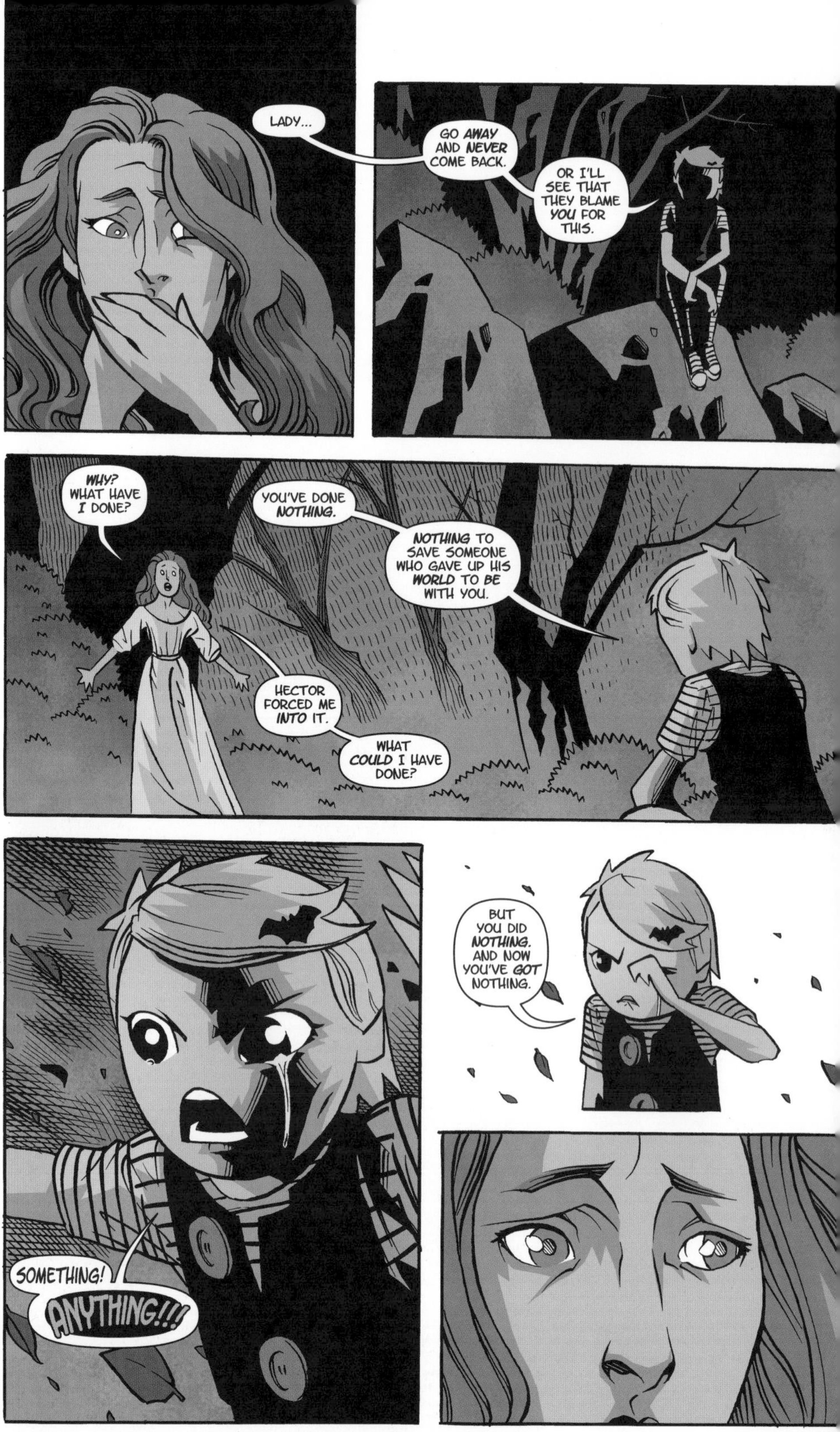
LADY...
GO AWAY AND NEVER COME BACK.
OR I'LL SEE THAT THEY BLAME YOU FOR THIS.
WHY? WHAT HAVE I DONE?
YOU'VE DONE NOTHING.
NOTHING TO SAVE SOMEONE WHO GAVE UP HIS WORLD TO BE WITH YOU.
HECTOR FORCED ME INTO IT.
WHAT COULD I HAVE DONE?
BUT YOU DID NOTHING. AND NOW YOU'VE GOT NOTHING.
SOMETHING!
ANYTHING!!!

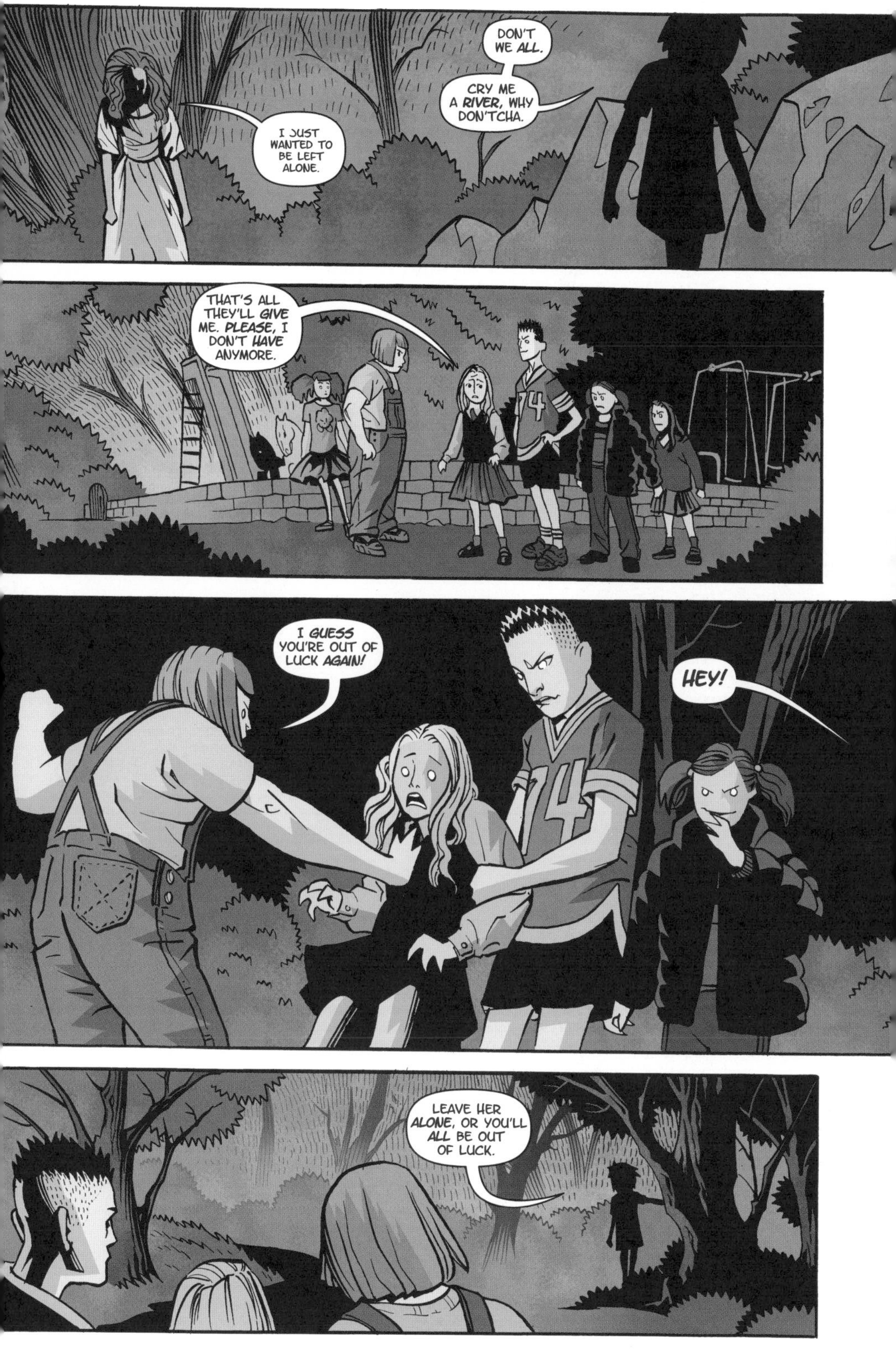
I JUST WANTED TO BE LEFT ALONE.
DON'T WE ALL.
CRY ME A RIVER, WHY DON'TCHA.
THAT'S ALL THEY'LL GIVE ME. PLEASE, I DON'T HAVE ANYMORE.
I GUESS YOU'RE OUT OF LUCK AGAIN!
HEY!
LEAVE HER ALONE, OR YOU'LL ALL BE OUT OF LUCK.

WHAT'RE YOU GONNA DO ABOUT IT, SKINNY?

THAT'S CRUMRIN, REMEMBER?

OOOOH, I'M WETTING MYSELF.

WHAT'S SHE GONNA DO? GIVE US ALL NIGHTMARES?

YOU WANNA FIND OUT?

OH NO...

I'M SICK OF YOU GUYS.

I DON'T WANT TO HEAR ABOUT YOU BOTHERING PEOPLE ANYMORE.

IF I DO...

YOU'LL FIND OUT EXACTLY WHAT COURTNEY CRUMRIN CAN DO.

AND *THAT* WERE THE *WAY* OF IT.

NO ONE EVER *FOUND* WHAT BECOME OF OL' MARSHAL *HECTOR.*

AFTER 'IS *DISAPPEARANCE,* THEY FOUND SOME *MIGHTY* INCRIMINATIN' STUFF IN 'IS 'OME.

LOOKS LIKE PROFESSOR *CRUMRIN* WASN'T AS IRRATIONAL AS YOU *THOUGHT,* EH, WOODRUE?

POOR OL' *WOODRUE* DIDN'T COME OUT LOOKIN' TOO GOOD, *NEITHER.*

'COURSE THEY STILL HAD TO FILL THEM VACANT SEATS ON THE *COUNCIL.*

THEY *TRIED* ASKIN' OL' PROFESSOR *CRUMRIN,* FOR *SOME* SILLY REASON.

SLAMM!

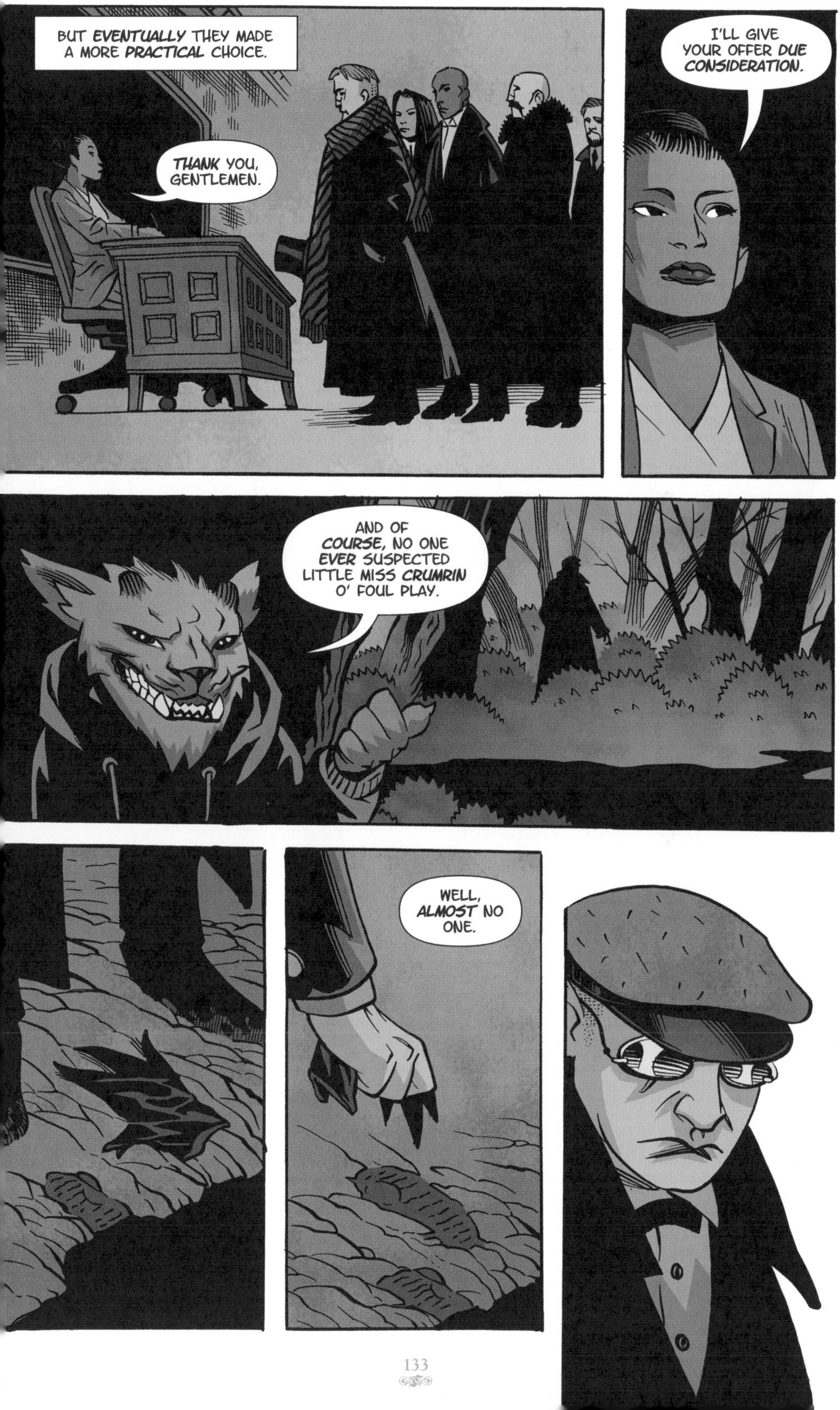
BUT EVENTUALLY THEY MADE A MORE PRACTICAL CHOICE.
THANK YOU, GENTLEMEN.
I'LL GIVE YOUR OFFER DUE CONSIDERATION.
AND OF COURSE, NO ONE EVER SUSPECTED LITTLE MISS CRUMRIN O' FOUL PLAY.
WELL, ALMOST NO ONE.

# Courtney

## VOLUME TWO

# Crumrin

## The Coven of Mystics

### Bonus Material & Cover Gallery

A pin-up drwaing of Courtney Crumrin drawn in 2009.

Original Cover for *Courtney Crumrin and the Coven of Mystics.*

Cover for the French Edition of *Courtney Crumrin and the Coven of Mystics.*

Cover for Issue 1 of *Courtney Crumrin and the Coven of Mystics*.

Cover for Issue 2 of *Courtney Crumrin and the Coven of Mystics*.

Cover for Issue 3 of *Courtney Crumrin and the Coven of Mystics.*

Cover for Issue 4 of *Courtney Crumrin and the Coven of Mystics.*

# TED NAIFEH

Ted Naifeh first appeared in the independent comics scene in 1999 as the artist for *Gloomcookie*, the goth romance comic he co-created with Serena Valentino for SLG Publishing. After a successful run, Ted decided to strike out on his own, writing and drawing *Courtney Crumrin and the Night Things*, a spooky children's fantasy series about a grumpy little girl and her adventures with her Warlock uncle.

Nominated for an Eisner Award for best limited series, Courtney Crumrin's success paved the way for *Polly and the Pirates*, another children's book, this time about a prim and proper girl kidnapped by pirates convinced she was the daughter of their long-lost queen.

Over the next few years, Ted wrote four volumes of *Courtney Crumrin*, plus a spin off book about her uncle. He also co-created *How Loathsome* with Tristan Crane, and illustrated two volumes of the videogame tie-in comic *Death Junior* with screenwriter Gary Whitta. More recently, he illustrated *The Good Neighbors*, a three volume graphic novel series written by *New York Times* best-selling author Holly Black, published by Scholastic.

In 2011, Ted wrote the sequel to *Polly and the Pirates*, and illustrated several *Batman* short stories for DC Comics. He is currently writing and illustrating the ongoing *Courtney Crumrin* series, which will celebrate its 10th year in 2012.

Ted lives in San Francisco, because he likes dreary weather.

# Courtney
### By Ted Naifeh
# Crumrin

## AVAILABLE NOW

**COURTNEY CRUMRIN, VOLUME 1:**
**THE NIGHT THINGS**
136 pages • 6"x9" Hardcover • Color
ISBN 978-1-934964-77-4

## COMING SOON

**COURTNEY CRUMRIN, VOLUME 3:**
**THE TWILIGHT KINGDOM**
136 pages • 6"x9" Hardcover • Color
ISBN 978-1-934964-86-6

**COURTNEY CRUMRIN, VOLUME 4:**
**MONSTROUS HOLIDAY**
136 pages • 6"x9" Hardcover • Color
ISBN 978-1-934964-92-7

**COURTNEY CRUMRIN TALES**
136 pages • 6"x9" Hardcover • Color
ISBN 978-1-62010-019-6

Look for the continuing adventures of *Courtney Crumrin* in
single issues at your local comic shop, in 2012!

## ALSO BY TED NAIFEH

**POLLY AND THE PIRATES, VOLUME 1**
By Ted Naifeh
176 pages • Digest • Black & White
ISBN 978-1-932664-46-1

**POLLY AND THE PIRATES, VOLUME 2**
By Ted Naifeh & Robbi Rodriguez
176 pages • Digest • Black & White
ISBN 978-1-934964-73-6

For more information on these and other fine Oni Press comic books and graphic
novels, visit www.onipress.com. To find a comic specialty store in your area,
call 1-888-COMICBOOK or visit www.comicshops.us.

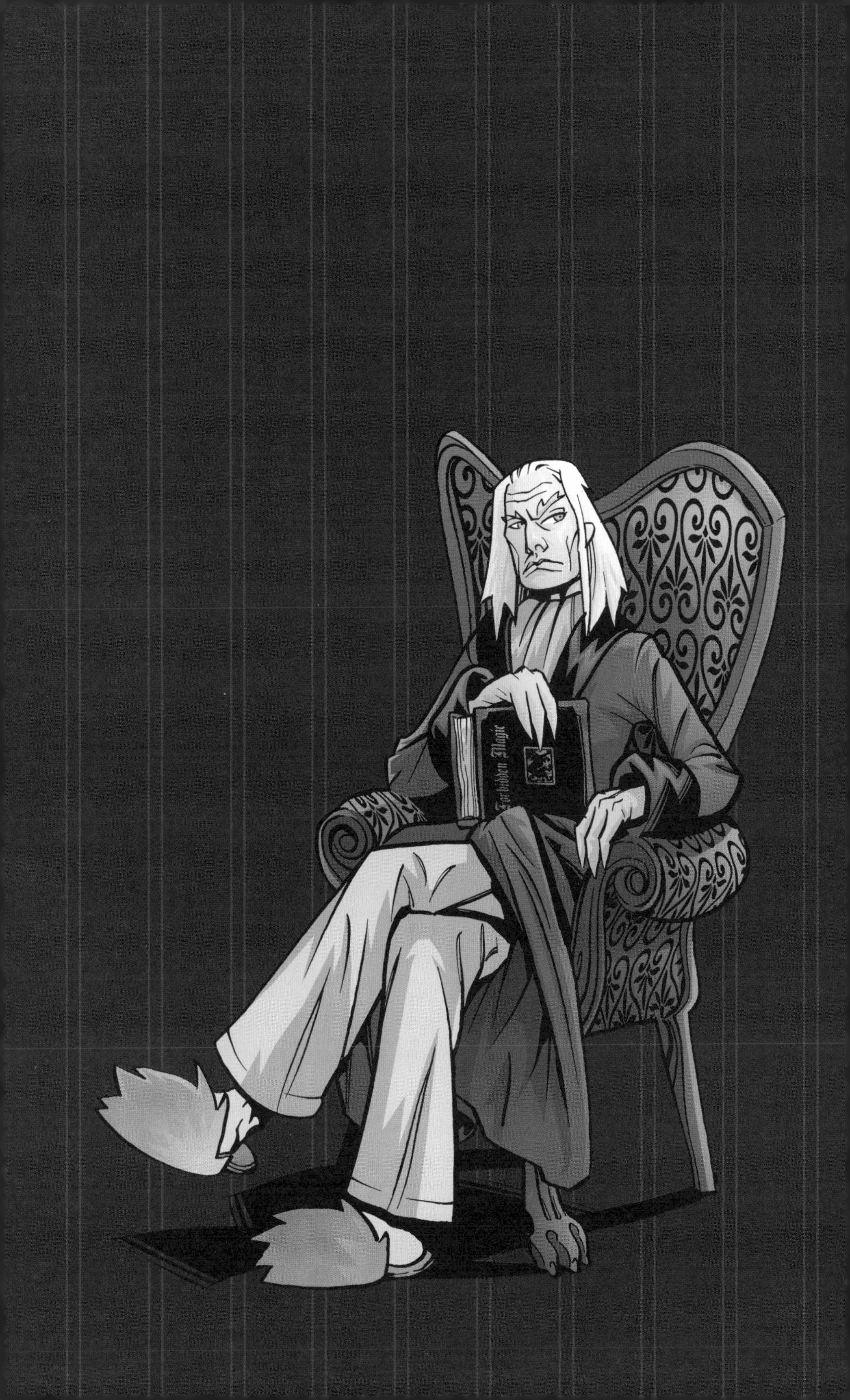
Forbidden Magic